THE TREES WITH FIVE LEAVES
BY
ARIAN ZENE

In memory of my beloved father. There are a couple of events and names, based on the true stories told by my father. I also dedicate this book to my son, Arlen and to all the kids in the world.

CHAPTER 1

Arl woke up earlier than usual. He washed, brushed his teeth and instead of eating breakfast slowly like he usually did, causing his mother, Briza, to say, "Stop dawdling, Arl!" he gulped it down. Then he put on his clothes with a speed that surprised even him.

"Wow, I' m a lightingspeedman!" he said.

And usually, Briza would have to say, at least two or three times, "Come on, Arl, you're going to miss the bus!"

Today was different. It was the third week of June and it had been two weeks since school ended. Arl and his grandpa Toke were going to pay a visit to Mother Nature. They wanted to be away from everyday things, where few other people could be seen and heard. And where was that? Well...a small lake, a dirt road, and a forest nearby. And that was just part of the beautiful scenery. There were also a bunch of soft, round hills that surrounded the lake.

The lake had been created a long time ago from underground spring water, but now it depended only on the rain. One day, the water might pop up again like a big fountain, but it seemed like that would have to be a miracle, because there had been so much dry weather of lately. Shaped like a kidney, the lake was really a heart for the people of Krasta, the city where Arl was born and lived. It gave them a place to go to, have fun, have picnics and play games like baseball, softball, and toss horseshoes. From the northeast side of the lake, only two hundred feet away, was a forest of poplar and plane trees.

A dirt road, extending three and half miles from the city of Krasta, separated the lake and the forest. This road branched out from the main asphalt road just outside the city. Cypress trees, which looked like antique statues of goddesses with their straight trunks, stood tall and proud on each side of the this dirt road

It was a long time since Arl had been at the lake. He had been busy with school, and also, his dad, Kent, was on a job assignment in another state, where he was on a geology expedition, trying to find some rare fossils. That doubled his mom's work, making less free time for her, and Grandpa Toke wasn't getting any younger. Arl's Grandma Elise, as they told Arl when he was in preschool, had gone to the sky, in a special place, and they were going to meet together again someday. At first, Arl was very angry and couldn't understand why she had left them, but as time went by, the anger passed and he just missed his grandma a lot. But when he mentioned her, he always looked up toward Heaven and was sure she heard him.

So that day, Grandpa Toke was ready to go. He had everything in order: his cooler so that the drinking water would keep cool, his tackle box that he got after he retired, and his heart medication. Before, he had liked hunting, but now fishing suited him better, and he even started to enjoy it.

One more time, Briza checked the things they were going to take, and gave the usual advice:

"Don't do that…careful about this, do that," and on and on and on. "I know, I know," said Arl.

"Oh you think you know everything now. You have two digits; you're a big man," continued Arl's mom.

Arl, who had turned ten in October, tried to act like an older boy. He was of average height and he was growing really fast. He was doing things for himself more often, starting with combing his medium-cut black hair, paying attention to clothes, using his dad's cologne, and so on, wanting to impress the girls! Lately, he had been getting into more serious conversations, such as about "climate change" and conservation, and environmental issues.

"Come on! Leave the boy alone. He is my buddy," said Grandpa, always trying to smooth things out. "You worry too much, Briza. He is a very good boy.

He's going to listen to me," and he ruffled Arl's hair with his fingers.

Briza looked at Arl, smiled a bit, kissed him in the forehead and the bottom of his chin and said "goodbye" to them. Arl fixed his backpack, helped Grandpa put his backpack on his shoulder, and then raised his hand, saying again goodbye to his mother. "Don't worry, Mom, everything is going to be fine," he said, and started to walk faster.

"Wait for me, Arl. See you later Briza," said Grandpa making a squeaky noise closing the big metal outside door.

CHAPTER 2

As Arl and Grandpa walked on, the city of Krasta was looking further and further and in the distance on that beautiful morning. Krasta is surrounded by soft, beautiful hills, and is known for the picturesque view, especially the old part of town with the houses painted in earth tones and red tiled roofs. From a distance, the houses look like they sit on top of each other. The streets are not that wide inside the town, and they curve and twist a lot, like veins in the lungs. Arl and his friends loved these streets a lot, especially when they rode their bikes.

Walking downhill, Arl and Grandpa left the city in a few minutes. They took a shortcut: a dirt road that people take when they go to the forest or lake. Time after time, Arl turned his head to see how far they had gone. The loud sounds of cars and city noises were being replaced by the gentle sounds of Nature. Arl was growing happier and happier as they got closer to the forest. He could hear the birds' songs, sounding sweeter and sweeter. He put one hand behind his right ear in order to be able to distinguish the sounds from each other: different sounds from the birds, the bees and hornets. Here and there, they heard a frog croaking: "croak, croak, croak." Arl translated that as "jump jump, jump" and he started jumping like a frog. Actually, it looked more like a rabbit jump, but that was OK. Arl was having fun being silly, and Grandpa Toke had a big smile of joy on his face, watching his grandson having fun.

Then Arl came close to Grandpa, grabbed his hand, and they continued to walk, growing smaller and smaller on the dirt road, looking like two dots on a giant snake.

"Grandpa Toke, which is your favorite animal?" asked Arl.

Grandpa walked a couple of steps and stopped, looking into the air as though he was going to find the story written there.

"Well, I was born in a village in a mountainside; you might know some of this already. We had some small livestock. Then, when I was still a young boy, my family moved to the city, and my contact with the animals was very limited, except during hunting trips."

Breathing a little heavily, he continued, "I love all the animals, but I can't forget a horse that saved my life."

"Tell me, G.T., tell me!" insisted Arl, walking backwards in front of his grandfather, whom he sometimes called G.T., short for Grandpa Toke.

"I was in the beginning of my military career and one of my duties was being a courier, and I had to ride a horse on many occasions; the same horse each time. He was a big horse, yet elegant; brownish with a white mark on his forehead and the bottom of his legs. He was a hunter breed and he had a perfect personality for this purpose. We called him Mezi. He didn't look that friendly in the beginning. It looked like he was saying, "Hey, human, use me and leave me alone. Throw me some corn, then leave." But one day, I was galloping through a forest trail, when suddenly something got caught on my neck and threw me onto the ground like a sack of potatoes. I was knocked unconscious and when I woke up, I felt something warm and wet on my face. I opened my eyes and saw a big, long face with two large nostrils that were breathing and releasing air right into my face. Things were clearing out in my head. I removed a broken phone cable, which apparently had thrown me to the ground, and then I realized I couldn't get up. "What am I going to do?" I asked myself. Horses, like humans, have five main senses: seeing, hearing, feeling, smelling and tasting, but some people think that they also have a "sixth" sense. That is their ability to sense danger, weather changes, and somehow to pick-up on human feelings. Mezi lowered his neck and tried to push me with his head, but when he saw that I couldn't get up, he bent his front legs, then the back ones, bringing his back very low. That helped me get slowly onto his back and he took me straight back to the military base where I got help from my friends

"After that, I treated the horse like a friend. I spoke to him, shared my thoughts, and sometimes he shook his head and neighed like he agreed with me, which was better than Grandma. She didn't agree all the time. Ho, ho, ho," echoed Grandpa's laugh in the forest.

Listening to the story about the horse, Arl hadn't realized that they had gotten close to the lake. "Now it's time for a break," said G.T.

"Why don't you tell me another story, G. T? Tell me the story of Kodhol, the baby ram you used to play with when you were a little boy like me. I like those stories," said Arl, trying to convince Grandpa.

"I have a better idea," said G.T. "I'll sit here by the lake and get ready for fishing, and you look around.

Maybe you can find some dry branches so we can make a fire together later on. How does that sound?"

"Oh, okay," said Arl. He was a little disappointed, but he liked exploring the forest, too, so he left his backpack on the ground, went to the lake, and splashed water on his face. "Oh, that feels good!" he said out loud, and then he started running. Pretty soon, he disappeared into the forest. He already felt the cool air in the shadows of the trees. "This is cool, for real," said Arl as the birds' songs and all the sounds of all the other inhabitants of the forest surrounded him.

Arl, delighted by the birds chirping, was making circles, with his head up, trying to find them between the branches of the trees. Who were those beautiful singers? Accidentally, he stepped on a branch that broke with a dry noise. "Oh, I totally forgot about picking up dry branches for the fire," said Arl and he started to look around.

"There is one. Here are some more." In a short time, he got enough dry branches for a fire. "I'll get a few more; then I'll get back to Grandpa," and he walked away toward a small hill. As he got closer, something unusual grabbed his attention. "Hmm, look at those trees. I've never seen trees like these anywhere," he said aware that no one but the birds and small animals in the forest could hear him. "Well, I am too young to know everything. Maybe that's how they are. They have four branches; one leaf on each of them, and another leaf all the way on the round top of a thick trunk. Poor trees," said Arl. "Maybe they don't have enough food and water. Maybe the water doesn't reach this high spot to grow more leaves or even fruits. But water reaches them when it rains, so I don't understand. Oh well, I better go back to Grandpa. He's going to get worried." Grabbing the pile of branches and leaving with a puzzled face, Arl thought, '*big trunk, no leaves. Well, only a few. How come?*' With these questions in his mind, Arl went back to where Grandpa was waiting for him.

"Is everything all right?" asked Grandpa. "Maybe a squirrel scared you or a groundhog," he joked and laughed, his shoulders moving up and down.

"Everything is OK, Grandpa. I just saw some strange trees or maybe they seemed strange to me," said Arl. He grabbed some branches and put them in order, pointing in one direction to help Grandpa make a fire later on. Then Arl started to throw some pebbles on the lake's surface. He tried to find them as flat as possible, so they could skim the surface, making a lot of circles.

"You're going to scare my fish," joked Grandpa as he handed the fishing rod to Arl. Arl held the fishing rod for a while, and Grandpa started preparing lunch. Together they made a big, noisy fire, which looked more beautiful by the lake. They sat around it, ate a couple of sandwiches and roasted some marshmallows. G.T. told more stories and Arl enjoyed listening, but time after time his mind went back to those strange trees he had seen earlier.

The sun was going down. The lake suddenly looked like a magic red carpet, decorated with little waves created by a light wind.

"I guess it's time to head back home. Let the lake sleep," said G.T. And he continued, "I asked an owl, 'O prince of darkness, can you keep one eye on the forest and one on the lake?' and he replied, 'With pleasure, my lord.' G.T. bowed like an old prince, followed by a laugh, then a cough and shortness of breath. "Oh, I am too old for this."

Arl giggled, too. They put out the fire, got their bags ready and slowly started heading home. "It wasn't a good fishing day today," said Arl, a little disappointed. I only caught two little trouts and I threw them back in the lake."

"We'll have better luck next time," said Grandpa. Arl nodded his head in agreement.

They walked quietly. The stars started to appear in the sky and the sun was changing shifts with the moon. Arl, looking up in the sky, started admiring the stars, thinking how pretty they were, and how far away. He started wondering. "Is any other kid watching the sky like me from any other planet? Is any other planet out there that has people like us? If yes, what do they look like?" He had heard so many stories about them, but had never seen a real "alien," as they were called, or sometimes they were called "extraterrestrials." Arl had seen pictures that made them look like monsters; but sometimes, they looked nice and friendly. Whatever they were, they were very mysterious and interesting, and Arl was eager to know more about them.

With these questions in mind, Arl and Grandpa arrived home. They were tired, but happy, a little hungry, but full with fun. Arl hugged his mom, Briza. She scanned him from head to toe and asked him how the trip was, and as always, started giving orders. "Go wash up! Help set the table!" etc. Arl did everything his mom said, hugged Grandpa, and thanked him for the wonderful day he'd had. It didn't take long for him to fall asleep. G.T.

told all the information about the day to 'Queen' mom. She reminded him to take his medication and they also went to bed for the night.

CHAPTER 3

Arl slept like a baby. The next day, he woke up as usual, dragging himself to do the morning chores, but he was looking forward to telling his friends about his exciting, awesome trip. He finished his breakfast quickly, grabbed his bike and rushed to the house of his neighbor and friend, Angika. Arl rang the bell of the two-story house. He could hear the steps behind the door, making a scratchy sound on the paved entryway. Their houses were in "the old neighborhood," as it was called. The difference between the "old neighborhood" and the other part of the city was in the style and age of the houses.

These houses were almost one hundred years old, and had a Mediterranean charm to them. Most of them were two- story homes and the yards were surrounded by high brick fences, which make the streets look narrower. A large wooden or metal door was the entrance for each house. Here and there people squeezed in a garage. The new neighborhoods were built on flatter land after World War II. They were airier, with wider streets. The front yards were open, except for a white picket fence here and there.

"Good morning," said Arl.

"I knew it was you," said Angika in a melodic voice. A sunbeam lighted up her face when she opened the door. Angika had a sweet face, a mixture of an Asian beauty, a Native American, a Latino, and young girls from other cultures. Arl thought she was like honey that the bees created by collecting nectar from different flowers. Her hair was shiny black, and perfectly straight as though she flat ironed it every day. She had two beautiful long braids that hung down on both sides of her face and they tied up together behind her head. Arl thought she look like an ancient goddess.

"Beautiful day today," said Angika.

"Perfect for a bike ride," said Arl. "Get your bike and let's go to Zeke's. What do you think?"

"That sounds great. Let me tell my sister and I'll get my IPOD," said Angika. She went inside her house; then a few minutes later, they both got on their bikes and rode as fast as they could in the direction of the house of their friend Zeke, who lived just down the road.

"Do you remember how far Zeke's house used to seem?" asked Angika.

"Yes, I do," said Arl. "Especially when we were in kindergarten. We couldn't even reach the doorbell," Arl continued, while pushing a gold-plated doorbell.

"We used to pound on the door until we heard the dog barking, and then we ran terrified," said Angika, raising her hands and acting all scared.

"Yes, they were fun years for us," said Arl, scratching his head.

Arl, Angika, and Zeke had known each other since kindergarten and had been friends ever since. If Arl left the house without saying anything, his parents knew where he was going: first, to Angika's house, and then, to complete the trio, to redheaded Zeke.

"Hey, pals, did you hear the news yesterday?" asked Zeke as soon as he saw them.

"No, I didn't. I was on a trip with my grandpa," said Arl.

"Me neither. I was shopping all day with my big sister," said Angika.

"Sorry, Arl, I forgot to ask you. How was it? I am sure you had a good time," said Zeke.

"Yes, tell us," said anxiously Angika.

"It was awesome," said Arl. "But first tell me about the news."

"Oh, that! A few people saw some lights in the sky and some kind of object all lit up that was moving too fast, right in our neighborhood. The object got close to the ground, made some circles, and then disappeared in the sky again," said Zeke.

"Who were those people who saw it? Do we know any of them?" asked Arl.

"I don't think we know them. They were two farmers from different places, a photographer who was hanging around that area, and a fisherman by the lake. Actually, the fisherman had a clear view of this flying object. He said it was a silver color. It was diamond-shaped with a bright-yellow circle around it. "The flying object", said the fisherman, "made a couple of circles around the lake, then a couple more around the forest; it went down through the woods for a few seconds, and then it went back up. The yellow circle became white and in a second, the object became a dot in the sky". Then the fisherman went through the woods, very frightened, thinking he might see something, but there was nothing," finished Zeke.

"Wow. How did I miss all that? I was at the same lake, same forest, but..." and Arl paused.

"Different day," they all said together.

"Yes, no luck," said Zeke.

"Maybe the fisherman was daydreaming," said Angika.

"Yes, maybe," agreed Zeke, "but what about the other guys who saw the lights, too. They all had the daydreaming disease if there is such a thing."

"Well, I don't know. We all kind of want to hear or even be part of those make-believe stories. Back to earth, buddies. Why don't we grab our bikes, Zeke? Tell your parents that we're going for a ride," said Arl.

"Okay, in a flash. Where to?" asked Zeke.

"Prepare your wheels, buddies, we're going to the forest and the lake," said Arl, raising his hand as though he was holding a sword. "We might have a job to do. We might meet the fisherman, too. You never know," continued Arl.

Zeke rushed to his house and came back in a few minutes, pushing his bike.

"To the forest!" exclaimed everyone, each holding up their right hand.

The three friends zigzagged through the narrow streets in their neighborhood, and in a few minutes, they had reached the edge of the city. They left the asphalt road and made a right turn onto the dirt road

"Let's race each other," said Angika as soon as they hit the dirt road. Her long hair was waving in the air as she was speeding up. All three friends started to ride fast through the dirt road, leaving behind a thin tail of dust. After riding for a while, they stopped in a valley covered with flowers.

"Let's take a break," said Angika who wanted to look at all the colorful flowers, different kinds of butterflies, and that special green color that grass turns in the summer. All three friends jumped from their bikes and scattered around the valley.

"Is this a groundhog hole?" asked Zeke.

"I guess," said Arl.

"Nature is the best painter in the world," said Angika, whirling around, with her arms open like she was ready to fly. "Look at those flowers. Oh, I love violets. Look at the butterflies. You know what? I'm going to make a tiara. Are you two going to make one?"

Zeke and Arl looked at each other, as though trying to decide.

"Oh, why not? I'm going to make one for my mom," said Arl.

"I' m giving it to my sister," said Zeke, and both boys spread around.

"That's how you do it?" asked Arl, looking at Angika's tiara.

"It's little bit tricky, and you have to be very gentle with flowers. They're very delicate. And then you put it here," continued Angika, placing her tiara on her head."

"Now you look like Angel…ika. I'm going to put it here," said Arl. He put his tiara around his neck and Zeke did the same.

"You both look like Hawaiian boys," laughed Angika. "Okay, time for a "hula dance," she said as she started to imitate the Hawaiian girls.

"I am a little rusty," said Zeke.

"Me too," followed Arl. Both boys seemed a little embarrassed.

"Come on, who's going to judge you in the middle of nowhere, the birds or that gecko I saw earlier?" joked Angika. Arl and Zeke exchanged glances again and both exhaled "Girrrrrls!" Then they hopped on their bikes again and continued riding, each singing a separate song in their head. As soon as they took another turn, they couldn't miss the reflection of the sunlight on the lake as if someone had thrown gold dust on the surface.

"Wow!" exclaimed Angika and Zeke at the same time.

"That's supernatural! Maybe that's why orbit flyers choose the lake," added Zeke.

"Could be," said Arl, "but let's get back to earth again. The reason I brought you here – well, the first reason was to enjoy nature together, but another reason is that I wanted to show you something I couldn't get out of my mind."

Angika and Zeke looked at each other like the answer was written on their faces.

"Let me show you," said Arl. They rode a little further, and when they reached the forest, they stopped. Arl left his bike by a tree.

"This way," pointed Arl after looking around as though he wanted to make sure that he was pointing in the right direction. Angika and Zeke left their bikes by a bush and started to follow Arl.

"Look at those roots," said Zeke. "They're covered with ants. It must be an old tree."

"And the woodpecker is waiting for them," said Angika, looking up at the tree. They got close to a hillock and Arl stopped. "Look at those trees. For some reason, they touched me; I felt like they're asking for help. "Help us! We want to grow more leaves. We want to be like the others, please." That's why I wanted you to help me, help those trees," finished Arl.

"These trees are really strange looking," said Zeke. "These two dwarf branches look like somebody chopped them down. And that single leaf looks very lonely. How are we going to help the trees?" asked Angika, surprised.

"I guess we need a plan," suggested Zeke.

"Well, I think we should start by doing a little research about trees," said Arl.

"Yes, maybe we can find a clue. Are those trees natural like that or are they slowly dying?" questioned Zeke.

"I wouldn't know," said Angika, pulling the headphones off her head, and turning off the IPOD. "Darn it. I know a lot about songs and singers, but very little about trees, or nature for that matter."

"I am sure we'll come up with something positive," said Arl, feeling good about his friends' agreement to help. The three friends hopped on their bikes, and headed home, racing here and there.

CHAPTER 4

The three friends spend the next day glancing through books about trees, talking to adults. They did that carefully, so they didn't make people suspicious. It was their challenge and they wanted to keep it like that.

They met in the afternoon at a small park near their homes, and started to share their findings.

"What do we have?" asked Arl.

"From what I read," started Angika, opening a folded paper with some notes, "plants need water, mineral salts and foods such as carbohydrates. A big factor that influences plant growth is the amount of sunshine. Plants use their extensive root systems to take in water from the ground. Each root branches into a network of rootlets. Water enters the plant through its roots. A column of water moves up through the plant, from the roots right through the trunk or stem into leaves. In summer, plant growth is at its height. That's all I've got for now," finished Angika flipping her hair on her right shoulder.

Zeke followed. "The leaves are eaten by many animals, including worms, insects, slugs, snails, millipedes and woodlice. The caterpillars of moths and butterflies also eat them. Some trees are chopped down or eaten by grazing animals."

"And we're going to exclude any vandalism. I don't think anybody would do such a thing or would they?" asked Arl. Arl was impressed with the seriousness that his friends showed. Then he added, "My great grandpa, according to Grandpa, was a tree specialist, same as one of my dad's uncles who is no longer with us.

They worked mostly with olives and vineyards. That's how a book explains their job: Sometimes poles are cut from trees, and the trees can then re-sprout from the base to provide another crop of poles later. This is called coppicing."

"So, they were like tree surgeons," said Zeke.

"Something like that. But we can't do this job ourselves. Some trees and other plants loose their leaves all at once every year. Most lose their leaves in the fall, and remain bare through the winter, remaining largely dormant until the spring. I read that somewhere. We have to find out what's going on with our trees, with only five leaves in the summer. So let's start with an action plan," said Arl with a seriousness that made him seem ten years older. He picked up a stick and made three X's in the ground. Then he continued.

"Light, air, sun, *one*;

Water, *two*;

Ground, *three*.

"We see plenty of sunlight, so let's circle one X. The ground is good enough for other trees, so I guess it should be good enough for our trees, too. We circle the second X."

"So it comes down to one thing – water," said Angika.

"And animals" added Zeke.

"Water is very close. Maybe the position of the trees in a hillock makes it difficult to reach," said Arl.

"Plus it didn't rain a lot lately," added Zeke. "You can see the old line of the lake's level."

"So we've got a thirsty lake and thirsty trees," said Angika.

"Thirsty trees? I guess we do. One idea is to get some water from the lake. We can use buckets for that. Maybe that's going to help our trees until the next rain. As far as the animals, what do you think Zeke?" asked Arl.

"It seems that only these trees are suffering, at least in our forest. So it's not hard to build a fence around them to protect them from animals. As far as the ants and their cousins, we will take a close look to see if that's the case," responded Zeke without pausing.

"It sounds good. Tomorrow morning, we'll get ready to start. Deal?" asked Arl.

"Deal," responded Angika and Zeke, and all three friends made a vow with their palms on top of each other.

CHAPTER 5

The next day came pretty quickly. Arl couldn't wait to start the project with his friends. He started packing again.

"What are you up to?" asked Mom Briza.

"We're going to the forest again," said Arl.

"Weren't you in the forest yesterday? What's going on here? Can I have a clue?" asked Briza again.

"There are no clues or claws, Mom. We just love being there. It is so much fun and interesting. We want to learn more about nature. That's all. And we love riding our bikes on the dirt road," finished Arl.

"There better be no claws then. You take care of each other, stay together and take care of Angika," said Mom Briza.

"Oh, she is stronger than us. She is a tough cookie," said Arl.

"Our kids are growing so fast," said Briza, looking at G.T., after Arl left to go to his room.

"We always think of our kids as smaller than they are. We want to keep them 'leashed' somehow. Let's release the 'leash' a little bit. There's more danger in the city than in the world of nature. Look at the statistics. Compare the number of car accidents with fishing or hunting accidents for that mater," said G.T.

"I know you're right, but I still can't help worrying a little," continued Briza. "Let's have some chamomile tea. It will calm my nerves."

"Sounds good," said G.T.

"Arl came out of the shed pulling a cart that held a bucket, some ropes and wires. He added the lunch bag, mounted his bike and headed down Angika's house.

"Hey, Angika," called Arl.

Angika appeared on at the window, waving at Arl.

"Are you ready?" asked Arl. Angika made the universal sign raising her pointing finger, meaning that she would be out in just a minute.

"Hmm, you are early and fully loaded," said Angika, looking at Arl with his bike pulling a cart.

"Yes, I brought some stuff with me. What did you get?" asked Arl.

Angika pulled her bike. She already had installed a basket in front and a cargo rack in the back. She also had a bucket, a lunch bag, a couple of biology books, and some music accessories. She put on her headphones and turned on the IPOD. "Now, I am ready," said Angika.

"Oh, I see. You are overloaded. Let's go get Zeke now," said Arl, and both hurried toward Zeke's house. When they approached Zeke's house, they saw him waiting outside.

"You got up early, too? We couldn't sleep much, either. I see you got some wood sticks," said Angika after taking off her headphones.

"Yes, there were some leftovers in the garage. I asked my father if I could use them for a project. He said "yes, of course" but he asked me to be very careful so I don't get hurt. And I brought some bandages with me, too," said Zeke.

"Very well, we are good to go then. Is the team ready?" asked Arl.

"Yes, we are," said Angika and Zeke in a synchronized voice.

They hopped on their bikes, and started pedaling. Angika put the headphones on again, and said, "Let's be on our way!"

The boys looked at each other, smiling and shaking their heads. Arl said to Zeke, "At least she's not going to make us sing or do the hula dance. We're both terrible dancers."

Time was flying and so were they. They were riding, each lost in their thoughts and the lake was getting bigger and bigger in front of their eyes. Arl's heart started to beat faster like it did before a big science test in school, but instead of a teacher checking the results, now the results were going to test him and his friends. The role of the teacher was going to be replaced by another judge named Mother Nature.

With those things in mind Arl and his friends arrived at the lake. Just by looking at the lake friends started to fill cooler, bringing down the heat and heavy breathing from the long ride. The sound of waives were like a relaxation, at least for the boys, Angika still had the headphones on. They got off their bikes, stretched a little, and started to unload their stuff from their bikes.

"I love the sounds," said Zeke, standing still, and turning his head so he could hear better.

"And the breeze" added Arl. "First, we start with water. What do you think?" Arl asked impatiently.

"OK," said Zeke. "But before we start watering, we can take a closer look for worms, insects, or a clue of anything else that might damage those trees."

"Good point," said Angika, taking her headphones off for a second.

"Point taken. So let's get straight to the *point*," said Arl, *pointing* in the direction of the forest. The three friends started laughing with the *pointy* conversation. They always played games with words. They filled their buckets with water from the lake and started to walk toward the forest. Arl was proud, excited, and worried all at the same time. He and his friends had taken the project into their own hands, without direct help from grownups. They were taking a chance even if they knew their actions were simple. But at least it was a start.

They got closer to the *five leaves trees;* that's what they were calling them lately, because of how they looked. They stopped and started to observe the trees again. All three looked the same, with two dwarf branches: two on the left, and two on the right side of the trunk, each ending with a single leaf. Obviously, the trees didn't grow more branches or leaves, but at the same time, they weren't losing any. The kids didn't find anything that looked like those trees in the books. The roots were exposed in a uniform way, so basically they looked the same, except for their height. They left their buckets by the trees, and started to investigate each tree from the roots to the top for any clue that was related to animals or insects damage.

Suddenly, Angika jumped off the ground. With both hands, she quickly pulled the headphones off her head.

"What's wrong," asked Zeke? "You don't like the music?"

"The music stopped," responded Angika, "and I heard some sharp noises. I can't compare them with any kind of music. It was very sharp. Instantly, it felt like my ears were going to explode," she continued, breathing heavily.

"Don't worry," said Zeke. "The signals are weak in the forest, sound waves crash in the trees, mix with other sounds, and create strange sounds," continued Zeke looking at Arl with a face that said, "Am I making any sense or not?"

"Maybe the IPOD broke," said Arl, and he went and grabbed his bucket, trying to remind his friends to get back to their main goal. "We don't see anything suspicious, so let's start with water." Arl dumped his bucket with water. Zeke and Angika dumped their buckets too, and they all headed back to the lake to fill them again. They raced each other down to the lake. Angika was the first. When Arl and Zeke came close, she started splashing them with water. It didn't take long. The three of them were splashing each other filling the air with shiny water sparkles and laughing cheers.

"It's time for a second trip, pals. What do you think?" asked Arl, "We got wet already. Let's get those trees wet, too," and he grabbed his bucket again and started to walk toward the forest, followed by Zeke and Angika. Angika put the headphones on again.

"Oh, it works now," said Angika, raising both hands.

Soon, they arrived by the trees, and all three friends froze when they looked down in the ground.

"This is as dry as it can be," said Arl.

"We already dumped three buckets of water, where did it go?" questioned Angika.

"I guess we need to take a few more trips with buckets," continued Arl, losing his confidence a little bit.

"We're not giving up," followed Zeke.

"We're going to try our best," added Angika. "And we'll ask for help from adults if we have to."

"Let's not lose our hopes for now," said Arl grabbing his bucket, "Let's count to three, and we'll

empty our buckets at same time. Three, two, one. Go!"
And they each emptied their buckets to the last drop.
Suddenly, Angika threw the bucket away as if it burned
her hand.

"What happened?" asked Zeke.

"I tried the IPOD earlier. It was fine, and I was
listening to the music again, but as soon as we dumped

the water on the roots, I heard the same weird noises, even stronger this time, like an entire band was playing inside my head," said Angika, looking around and up in the air, trying to find the answer.

"That is weird," said Arl.

"And this is weirder," added Zeke pointing at the ground nearby the trees. The wet dirt was drying really fast, sucking the water right in front of their eyes. Was that the reason why those trees weren't growing normally? Probably, they couldn't get enough water. Or? With that question in mind, Arl addressed his friends: "Let's keep going. Time will tell us everything," and he ran to the lake again.

"I'll go after you," said Zeke to Angika.

They got close to the lake without saying a word, like they didn't want to break the silence. It seemed like it was better being in a silence mode, than hearing an unknown strange, eerie sound.

"We'll take a break, and then we'll go back to the forest," said Arl, breaking the silence. "And, Angika, I suggest, that you don't use the headphones for a while." He was acting like a big brother.

"You're right. I better sing myself," responded Angika.

"Just, please, not out loud. You're going to scare the birds away, but the fish are safe, they can't hear you" joked Zeke, and both friends started laughing more than usual, like they wanted to compensate for the earlier eerie moments.

"Oh, really? You are worried about the birds? Then, I'll bring you a *hello* from the fish," and she started the splashing game again.

Cheerful voices filled the air. The friends got wet again, but they didn't forget that the tree trunks were still dry and thirsty.

"Before we go again, let's eat something," proposed Arl.

"It sounds just about right," said Angika. "I brought with me some homemade cookies that I baked myself, so let's see how you like them when you taste the cookies. She opened her lunch bag, then a plastic container, and she gave both of them a couple of light-brown cookies.

"Oh, heaven!" said Zeke after he tasted the cookie, closing his eyes.

"These are close to my grandma's cookies. The future of cuisine is in good hands. I give you *THE BEST*

COOK award," said Arl, and grabbed a tiny flower that was hiding between the rocks, and gave it to her.

.   "Oh, stop it," said with a smile flattered Angika. Friends were enjoying their food and soon, they got lost in their thoughts. It didn't take long, and Arl got up.

"What's wrong?" asked Zeke.

"Nothing," responded Arl. "You two stay a little bit longer. I am going to check what's going on in the forest, and I'll be back pretty soon."

"I'm coming too," said Zeke. "I am done with my food. I wasn't that hungry anyway." Zeke got up from the stone he was sitting on.

"No. You stay with Angika," insisted Arl. "We'll go together later for watering and building the fence," and he started to walk away as he was finishing the sentence. He was feeling a little guilty that he had brought his friends along and put them to work. At the same time, he knew that his friends would always back him up for doing the right thing. When he arrived there by the trees, Arl was almost running. He needed an answer very badly. He wished he knew more about trees and greenery, in general. He felt bad for those trees. He wanted to take care of them like they were little puppies or kittens.

CHAPTER 6

The first thing Arl saw was the dry ground again. He sat on his knees and touched the ground with one hand like he wanted to feel something. Then, he touched one of the exposed roots. As soon as he did that, there was a weird sound, coming from inside the tree. It seemed like something was moving there, from the roots below and moving up to the top. Arl raised his head, following the sound, and suddenly he just froze up. Above his head, in one of the branches, he saw a round blue object, which was changing colors just before his eyes. It became brown, then green, and finally, the color changed to red. Arl got up to take a better look. Maybe he was imagining things. What he saw was a round red object on top of one the trees. This tree was the tallest and widest of all three of them.

"Wow!" exclaimed Arl. "How did this happen? Is this supposed to be a fruit or something? That would be awesome, so our hard work hasn't been wasted. But fruits don't just appear from nowhere. I can't wait to tell Zeke and Angika about this." Arl was really stunned and happy. He couldn't believe it. Grandpa Toke and his parents were going to be very proud of him and his friends. Arl, Angika and Zeke were trying to save those trees, and the trees were thanking them with fruits. Nothing could beat that. To confirm his magic thoughts, Arl raised one hand to touch the fruit and hold it for a while, like he was holding a trophy. He closed his eyes, and started to use his imagination. "And the trophy for the *LIVE FOR LEAVES AWARD* goes to the young team

3 G's, which stands for *GET GREENER GOAL.*"
Whistles, cheers, applause. "That must be a cool award, named LFL; *LIVE FOR LEAVES*," said Arl, "and I am going to propose the name "3G" to my friends. This is one of the nicest daydreams, I've ever had," concluded Arl as his fingers approached the strange red fruit. But just before he was going to grab it, he felt an air pressure against his body that he couldn't resist, and it pushed him backwards. He became unconscious.

Angika and Zeke had already finished their food and were throwing pebbles in the lake to see who was going to make more circles at the surface. They played this game all the time and loved it, especially Zeke. He was the best at it.

"I think Arl is taking too long," said Angika, looking at the pebble making leaps on the surface of the water like a happy frog. "We better go check him out."

"He said he was coming back shortly," said Zeke, and he didn't throw the stone that he had in his hand. Instead he left it were he had gotten it. "We better fill those buckets with water, too, so we don't go there empty-handed" Zeke grabbed his bucket, and started to fill it up. Angika did the same thing, and both started to walk toward the forest without saying a word. They looked at each other without saying a word and started to walk faster. Buckets were swinging left and right, and water was splashing around, but they didn't slow down. They entered the forest and both started to call "Arl, Arl, are you ok? Say something."

"No answer. Maybe he's playing a game?" said Angika. "No, he couldn't do that to us, especially under these circumstances" Angika answered herself.

"I am starting to have a weird feeling," said Zeke, starting to look around.

"Actually," continued Angika, "these weird things started happening to us from the beginning of this trip. I can mention the strange interruption in the headphones twice, funny looking trees, and who knows what else lies ahead. There are the trees by the way, but no sign of Arl around," finished Angika. They both started to shout really loud, "Arl, where are you, please answer," and they started to run toward the trees. Angika left her bucket on the ground.

"The trees look the same, the ground is dry, but where is Arl?" Zeke left his bucket on the ground too, and started to look around again for a clue, for a little sign. "Arl, Arl!" They continued calling him until they heard something. They turned their heads in that direction. A bush moved like wind was blowing on it. Nothing else was moving.

"Let's check it out," said Zeke and both of them walked carefully on their tiptoes toward the bush. They were breathing through their nose like they didn't want to scare away what was there. Even the birds stopped singing for a moment. They separated; Angika went left, Zeke on the right side of the bush. "Frap, frap, frap." A bird flew from inside the bush, flapping its wings really fast. Both Zeke and Angika backed up one step, leaning backwards.

"Huh?" said Angika. "My heart is pounding really fast," and she sat on her knees.

"That's all it was, a bird?" said Zeke. "Let's check behind the bush. I don't think a bird can move the whole bush," continued Zeke as he took three more steps around. And he stopped with his eyes wide open. "There's Arl, Angika. I think he fell asleep. Arl, wake up!" said Zeke, shaking Arl's shoulder.

"Is he hurt?" asked Angika, bending over Arl. Soon, a teardrop fell from Angika's eyes and landed on Arl's left cheek, then another one. Angika was crying quietly. As the third drop was going down, Arl blinked his eyes. He sat up.

"What happened? Where are we? What are you two doing here?" He looked at Angika's eyes? "Are you crying, Angika?" he asked. "What happened, are you both okay?" And he looked at Zeke for an answer.

"You scared us to death," said Zeke. "We waited and waited, and then we decided to look for you, to see what was keeping you here."

Arl was listening, and at the same time trying to remember what happened to him. What made him fall down behind the bush? Who or what pushed him, that made him fall? What did he do before that? What did he see? What did he touch?

"Wait a minute," thought Arl. "I was trying to touch a fruit, *the fruit*. Now everything is coming together like a puzzle." The excitement came back. "Hey," he said, you're not going to believe what I saw. You are going to be very happy and proud." He got up very quickly. "Let me show you," and Arl walked toward the tree that had the fruit. Angika and Zeke followed him without saying a word, like they were hypnotized.

"We got served with a *fr...*" Arl couldn't finish his sentence as he was pointing at one of the tree branches. He just stood there for a few seconds, then after he took a look around, turning his head left and right, he continued: "Right on this branch, I saw a nice round, red fruit. I almost touched it."

"A fruit? Cool, then where is it?" asked Angika. She kept looking at Arl and Zeke simultaneously.

"Yes, Arl, where is it? Did it fall down on the ground somehow?" questioned Zeke, who started to look on the ground around the trees.

"I wanted to touch it, feel it," continued Arl. "Then this air pressure pushed me away from it, and the next thing I saw, was you," finished Arl. Zeke looked at Angika. Then he whispered, "Is *he daydreaming or are we all e daydreaming?*"

Angika raised her shoulders. "Okay," she said. "Let's think it over. You came here and saw this red round thing hanging on one of the branches. That must have been a fruit. Then something pushed you, but you didn't see what or who did it, and you ended up unconscious a few feet away, behind the bush. Now the fruit is gone, like it never existed," finished Angika as she covered her lips with her left forefinger.

"So, you saw the fruit," continued Zeke, "something pushed you and you fell asleep. Then you wake up and the fruit is gone. Either that thing that pushed you took the fruit or when you were asleep, an animal or a *ghost* got it."

"We definitely have to build that fence," said Arl, "just to make sure no animal can get close to the trees.

As far as birds, we'll take our chances. So, let's start

before it gets dark."

CHAPTER 7

Angika and Zeke looked at each other, and both raised their shoulders. They dumped their buckets again, still witnessing the ground getting dry really quick in front of their eyes. They left their buckets by the trees, and all three friends started to go toward the lake. When they arrived there, Arl splashed his face with water, like he wanted to wash off his early strange memories. But the memories were piled up in his head, so all he could do was sort them out. He was trying to figure out what had happened, what else can they do, etc.

They grabbed whatever they needed. Zeke got the wood sticks under his arm. Arl used his bucket to put the ropes and some other tools in it.

Zeke interrupted Arl's thinking. "Arl, don't hold anything, you must be hurt. Angika and I can handle it."

"No, I am fine, I actually feel really good after that nap or whatever we want to call it," said Arl. Angika and Zeke looked at each other, but they didn't say anything. Arl seemed okay, didn't have any bruises or any other signs of being hurt, so there was nothing to worry about for now, except they had to hurry before it got dark. They had to build that fence the best that they could, go home, get some really good sleep, and hope that a new day was going to bring them new ideas or better news. They soon arrived at the trees, and put the tools on the ground. Arl grabbed a stick and drew a circle with it, surrounding the *five leaves trees*. He looked at them and he was thinking; "*all three trees look the same, except for the height and width. Humans and animals have twins, triplets, quadruplets, quintuplets etc., but our friends never saw or heard about identical plants or greens. Similar? Yes, but not identical."*

"Let's start making some holes in the ground. We'll put the sticks in them, and tie them up with each other," said Arl, trying to sound confident, but all he knew was from some classes he had taken about the history of boats, from ancient times to the present. The lessons were simple, easy for kids to understand. The teacher had shown a film about how humans built a raft or a ferryboat to travel on water. Even the ropes came from tree: no metal or other material involved. Arl recalled the teacher saying, "If you lift up a raft, it's going to look like a wooden fence. So, in the 21st century, we are repeating the same methods that were being used thousands of years ago. In the end, continued the teacher, nature didn't change as much as humans. Nature always gave us everything we needed, but humans want more and more." Arl scratched his head as he thought about the teacher's words, now. There were many things about life on Earth that Arl couldn't understand. This was one of those things. Maybe he would understand when he was older, he hoped.

As they started to make holes in the ground, they heard strange, deep, squeaky noises that seemed to be coming from underground. The three friends stopped and just listened, cupping their ears with their hands in an effort to hear better. The noises continued for a few more seconds and then stopped. The children looked at each other for an answer. They were a little scared. It was a sure thing they heard something, but that something didn't have a name.

"There's nothing to worry about," said Arl. "The sounds are far away, but the ground distributed them. In different areas of the world, tribes or people, including Native Americans, used to put one ear close to the ground, trying to catch sounds. That showed them if something was moving, what direction it was moving in, so they could get prepared, or for whatever reason. Since we are really close to the ground's surface, that might be the case," said Arl, trying to convince himself first, and then his friends. Angika and Zeke raised their hands hesitatingly.

They continued building the fence and they didn't hear the weird sounds again. Finally, they were done and very happy with the results. The fence wasn't that big, only two feet high, but enough to keep animals away.

"Let's hope squirrels won't get attracted to our trees," said Zeke. "I guess our job for today is done."

"We have one more thing to do," said Angika.

"What?" asked Arl and Zeke at the same time, looking around trying to find something they might have missed.

"We have to ride our bikes home fast before we fall asleep on them," continued Angika, sounding exhausted.

"Oh, that job. We'll take care of that," said Zeke, smiling.

"We can put the tools inside the fence," said Arl. "I don't think the hooter or anything else is going to need them," joked Arl. The three of them agreed, and laughed at the same time.

"Goodnight, triplets. Sleep tight. Make some fruits for us tomorrow. Yes, at least three, one each. That's your homework." They were talking to the trees, as they were getting ready to go home.

They walked slowly down the slope, with mixed emotions. They felt good having finished the first day of work, for doing something to achieve their goal. They had gotten a little frightened from those strange sounds, but in the end, nothing happened. Arl, for some strange reason, felt better and more energized after the incident occurred. Definitely, they were going to give it one more try with water, and after that, maybe they would call for help from professionals. With these thoughts in mind, Arl and his friends got close to the lake, grabbed the rest of their things, put them on their bikes, and took a final glance at the lake. The color of the lake, which was a mixture of blue, green and gray, was getting darker, making a beautiful contrast with the red-golden sunbeams. This change of the lake's color and the sunbeams were like warning signs that the sun was going to leave pretty soon, which meant that it really was time to go home. They still had plenty of time to go home before dark. So they hopped onto their two wheelers and started riding in slow motion toward their cute little town.

All friends dwelled on their own thoughts. A couple of minutes went by, and Arl broke the silence. "You know, while I was enjoying, looking at the fruit earlier today, I was imagining us, with the fruit transforming into a trophy, like a team, receiving the best team award for a LIVE FOR LEAVES contest. Our team's name was 3Gs, which stands for GET GREENER GOAL. It felt really good, and it will be so cool if we really have a contest that involves a lot of kids, even teenagers and adults."

"Wow!" said Angika, and she stopped riding. Zeke and Arl stopped, too. "A 'LIVE FOR LEAVES' contest. 'GET GREENER GOAL'. That's really a cool daydream. And it will be cooler if we make it a reality. We can share this idea with other friends in the neighborhood and school. Actually, summer camps, too," continued Angika. Then she hopped onto her bike again, followed by her friends, and the wheels started to roll.

"A green contest. It looks like we're going to expand our adventure," said Zeke. He paused for a little, then he said, "It will be fun and for a good cause. It's not going to hurt anybody or anything. Before we only thought that we were going to play a game, but now we're going to try to combine that game with an activity that will help our neighborhood in one way or another. It will help our forest, our lake"

"Our planet!"Arl added excitedly. "You kids talked like real green heroes, like real 3Gs. So, what do you think? Did that daydream come for a reason, so we can be 3Gs? Maybe," Arl answered himself, "but it doesn't hurt to spread the word around. We can talk to our parents, and contact our teachers or even our principal."

"Aren't we exaggerating a little bit?" said Angika. "Then again, it doesn't hurt to share our ideas with others, especially if it's for a good cause."

This conversation gave the friends a little burst of energy and they started to ride their bikes faster. They were tired and couldn't joke like they did when they rode their bikes in the morning, or race each other either, for that matter. So most of the ride was quiet with a stop here and there for a sip of water or fix their things that might have moved from the little bumps in the dirt road.

It didn't take long for the first houses to appear on the horizon. Their cute little town was becoming less distant and clearer every minute. The threesome had just reached the asphalt road, which meant they were in the edge of their little city. Now they had to ride uphill, but the idea that they were getting closer to their houses made them ride faster. The first house to appear from the direction they were coming from was Angika's; two houses down was Arl's. The last one to arrive home, of course, was Zeke, whose house was just down the hill, a quarter of a mile from Arl's house.

"Okay *3G*'s, one *G* is leaving," said Angika, smiling as she approached her house. "I'll see you tomorrow at the same time. Bye pals."

"Bye, Angika," said both boys at the same time. "You did well," added Arl. Angika smiled again, waved her hand one more time and entered her house. Arl and Zeke walked toward Arl's house, pushing their bikes.

"Another *G* is leaving," said Arl, smiling at having used Angika's expression. "I'll see you tomorrow, buddy. Tomorrow, I'm going to bring the camera to take some pictures of our trees, so we can compare their appearances on different days. What do you think, Zeke?"

"That's a good idea. We should take a picture of the trees with ourselves in it, too," responded Zeke.

"You're right," said Arl. "A picture with our first project. Done." They shook hands. Zeke jumped on his bike and rode down the hill. He didn't have to move his pedals. The bike just seemed to move by itself as if it knew just where to go. Pretty soon, Zeke arrived at his house, put the bike aside and when he turned around, he almost fell down backward because his cute dog, that had so much hair one could hardly see his face, jumped up on him. Then from that gray ball of hair came a red tongue that started to lick Zeke's face really fast as though it was an ice cream cone. That was Zeke's dog, a Bergamasco, a herd-guard dog, but for Zeke, he was just a family dog, that he called Pepe. He had gotten Pepe for his tenth birthday. He promised his parents that he would take care of him, especially his unusual cord-like coat that required

a good deal of attention.

CHAPTER 8

Back at Arl's house, Arl was really happy. His mom told him the news that his dad's going to come home from his trip really soon, and best of all he was going to bring Arl some volcano stones, so Arl could add them to his stone collection. Arl remembered his first stone, which he found in a river, in the town where his uncle lived. The stone was shiny and Arl thought that he had found a treasure, like in the pirate stories. Well, for a five year old, it was a treasure. Since then, he collects stones everywhere he could. His dad, Kent, helped him to identify them.

Then, Arl told Grandpa Toke this account of the day's happenings – everything! Arl was half asleep when he took a shower, and he closed his eyes as soon as his head touched the pillow.

Morning came too fast. Arl didn't move an inch on his pillow. Most of the time, he moved around the bed like a clock hand, but the activities of the day before had drained his energy somewhat. He woke up later than usual, looked at the clock, and said, "Wow, what happened to me? I guess Angika and Zeke are both still asleep, since they haven't called me yet. I guess they are just tired like me. It is my fault. I made them do this, or I had the idea. Today we're going to make a good decision before we move on," said Arl, talking to himself.

"Decision, tired, move on, your fault. What's going on? Is everything okay?" asked Arl's mom, Briza.

"Nothing to worry about, Mom," replied Arl. "I'm just tired from riding my bike, that's all. But today will be the last trip for a while. We're going to take a break."

"You're going to go again? This is getting out of hand," said Briza, looking at GT. "You're going to take his side again?"

GT didn't say anything; he just motioned for her to calm down. "One more day," he said silently, "and Kent will be home. Then I will be able to relax more and let Kent help you deal with the problems of raising a child. I already had my turn raising my own."

"I thought kids would be easier to handle when they get older, but it seems different," continued Briza. "What am I saying? Anytime Kent goes out of town because of his job, I have to calm you down. So basically a parent is always a parent." She just started the routine again, making breakfast and packed Arl's lunch, and gave him the usual advice.

"Oh, I almost forgot the camera," said Arl, and he went to his room to get it. Briza looked at GT. GT raised his hands. "I don't know, just leave him alone."

Arl got the camera, put it in his backpack, and with his mouth full, rushed out the door. With one hand on the bike's steering bar, Arl walked to Angika's house. When he got ready to call her, she just opened the door, and he barely said "An...

"Are we late?" she asked.

"No, we don't have much to do today. We're going to throw some water on the tree roots again, and if nothing happens we'll take some pictures of the trees and show them to the biology teacher. Maybe he can give us a clue. I see you don't have your headphones today. You're not bringing them with you, I guess"

"It's not that much fun listening over there, plus it distracts me from concentrating on our job. I've got plenty of time to listen to music. Besides, there is the music of birds singing. Nobody can beat them, right?" said Angika. Then, they both jumped on their bikes, and rode toward Zeke's house. On their way there, they saw Zeke, who had a rope tied onto his bike. At the end of the rope, was this pile of hair that moved. He had his dog, Pepe, with him.

They played with him for a while. Pepe didn't stop shaking his tail with joy.

"You did good taking Pepe with you. He's going to cheer us up," said Angika.

"We're going to make him the 4th G," said Arl. "Actually, he is a G already. He never hurt a tree or polluted the water, nor the air. Even when he does his "business," it is good for nature, a little bit smelly though," continued Arl, laughing and looking at Pepe, who kept shaking his tail like he agreed. Pepe barked twice as though telling them, "That's human concerns, not my concerns. I've always been a dog. Nothing changed for me and my family, except we got a lot lazier and I don't see my cousins very often. And the cat next door hates me. I don't know why." Each friend translated Pepe's bark in their own version, but they all loved him.

They left the town, all falling in their own thoughts. They didn't feel the distance they had traveled. They stopped a couple of times. Pepe wanted to chase the butterflies, so Zeke released the leash, and they all enjoyed Pepe's chase, which was more of a game for the dog than a real goal. Then Zeke got the leash again, tied it to his bike and they continued on their adventure again.

CHAPTER 9

It didn't take too long for the kids to see the lake. Zeke took the leash off Pepe's neck, and you could see the joy of Pepe rushing toward the lake. As soon as he arrived, he jumped into the lake, made a couple of circles and got out. Then he started to shake his long hair, filling the air with water sparkles. Arl rushed with his bike, pulled out his camera, and took a couple of pictures of Pepe shaking his body, and that gave him a little shower in response.

"Now he's going to need all day to dry," said Zeke. "But that's okay. It's hot anyway, so that will cool him down." Zeke put the leash around Pepe's neck again. "Pepe and I are ready to go now."

"Let me wet my hair, too,"said Angika, and she bent down toward the surface of the lake, turned her head sideways, and her long, beautiful hair dipped into the water. Then, she twisted the hair for a few seconds, and she knew she wasn't going to use the hair dryer. She was going to use the sun dryer.

"Okay, it's the wet hair day," said Arl, and he wet his hair too, followed by Zeke. "Thanks for the tip, Pepe." Arl shook his head like Pepe, making Angika and Zeke laugh.

"Let's go cool off our friends with the five leaves now," said Arl. He left his bike and backpack like always, grabbed his camera, and started to walk toward the forest, followed by his friends and the hairy new member of his team. Walking mindlessly, and playing with Pepe, they got close to the hillock, where the *five leaves trees* home was.

"What happened with the fence?" exclaimed Arl, who ran toward the fence to get a better look. Angika followed behind Arl. Zeke wanted to run, too, but Pepe didn't want to move and started barking in the trees' direction.

"What's wrong, Pepe? You don't like our trees? Okay, I'll give you some time to get to know them," Zeke tied him up to a tiny tree close by, and ran to his friends.

"Part of the fence is torn down," said Arl, looking at Zeke with disappointment.

"Is that the same tree that produced the fruit?" asked Zeke.

"Yes," Arl replied.

"Well, the fence is only destroyed in front of that tree," Zeke pointed out. "Maybe another fruit appeared and somebody wanted to take it: an animal or a naughty kid."

"I don't know what to say," Said Arl, "but I know that our hard work didn't pay off. We have to ask for help. I'll just take a couple of pictures." After taking the pictures, Arl sat on the ground. Angika sat next to him, followed by Zeke. "Why you didn't bring Pepe here, Zeke?" asked Arl.

"He didn't want to get close to our trees, and he started barking strangely, so I thought I'd give him some time to relax," responded Zeke.

"Now he's barking again, but in a different direction," said Angika, and she got up to see what Pepe was barking about. Zeke got up quickly, and so did Arl.

"I don't see anything," said Angika.

"Me neither," said Zeke. "Maybe he is barking at something far from here. Dogs have a strong sense of smell."

Just then, a bolt of lighting flashed behind some big, tall trees. "Lighting in a blue sky? We don't want this now. But actually, we need it," said Angika. Zeke went by Pepe to calm him down.

"You're going to be a good weatherman – I mean weatherwoman," joked Zeke. The three were getting ready to leave, when they heard the sound of very strong wind, like when a tornado is coming. But it only lasted for a few seconds. They all turned their heads, and just like in a magic show, a boy appeared.

"Hello, my friends, how do you do?" greeted the boy.

The three friends were speechless for a moment. Then, to be gentle and not make the boy feel uncomfortable, Arl spoke first, "Oh, hi. My name is Arl. These are my friends Angika and Zeke."

"Hi," said Angika, waving her right hand.

"What is your name?" asked Zeke, staring at the boy.

"My name is Anzear," responded the boy, and he grabbed his braid that was hanging in front of his face, and flipped it on back of his head. His hair was medium-length referring to a girl's size. The hair was dark and straight on the bottom, and curly and light on the top of his head. His jacket had a modern cut, with a pointy collar, square shoulders and fake pockets. His pants were attached to his shoes, like they were one piece. Their color changed between blue and gray.

"Where are you from?" asked Angika. "I like fashion, but I never saw this style. That boy must be a foreigner," Angika whispered into Arl's ear.

"I am from far away," answered the new boy.

"How far?" asked Zeke, "Out of state or overseas?"

"Too far. I came here for a visit." The new boy paused for a short time. Then he said, "A visit from another town." He paused almost after every word. Anzear was staring at the kids, looking at them very carefully, one after the other, from the top of their head to the bottom of their feet. Then he turned his head and started to observe the dog. Pepe backed up a little and tried to hide his head between his front legs.

"This is my dog, Pepe," said Zeke.

"A dog!" said Anzear stretching the O. "This is cold!"

"My family and I take very good care of him. I tied him up because he was a little scared earlier, but most of the time, we unleash him," said Zeke. "A dog! Where he's from, he never saw a dog before in his life? Maybe he didn't. Who knows his story? Maybe I don't have to get angry at him, after all," whispered Zeke, and he pulled some treats from his pockets and gave them to Pepe.

Anzear didn't move an inch as he was looking at the treats, and how Pepe was grabbing them right from Zeke's hand. "Yes, he loves them," said Zeke. "Now I am convinced that the new boy had never seen a dog in his life."

"Are you alone or with somebody else?" asked Arl. "You can hang out with us for a while if you want to."

"I have two other friends," said Anzear. "Who is going to get hanged?" asked Anzear, alarmed.

"Nobody," said Arl smiling. "I meant do you want to stay with us for a while."

"For a while? Sure," said Anzear, still pausing after each word.

"We had a project going on. Let us show you," said Arl, and he started to walk toward the *unusual trees*. "Come on friends, let's fix the fence, and decide what to do after that." Angika and Zeke followed Arl. Anzear made a military turn, and he also followed the others.

"You like the music, yes?" Anzear said to Angika.

"Yes, most of the people like the music," responded Angika. "I guess you like it, too. What kind of music do you like?

"I like *hip*," answered Anzear.

"You mean *hippy?* Why do you like that?"

"I like that because you hop, hip-hop," said Anzear, and he started to jump up and down like he had springs in his legs.

"OH, I get it. You like hip-hop," said Angika. The three kids started to laugh out loud, but they stopped shortly. They didn't want to make their new friend feel uncomfortable and embarrassed. Actually, Anzear didn't mind at all.

"This is cold," he said. "I like it."

"Sorry, we got carried away," said Arl.

"You are always not happy by the trees. Today, I make you happy. I feel good. But that is not good," said Anzear, pointing at broken fence.

"Yes, as you can see, the other trees have plenty of leaves. Those three have only five. We wanted to do something to help those trees grow more leaves like the rest of the trees in the forest, but so far, nothing has helped. Now we've got a broken fence. That breaks our hearts. After all, we feel good because we tried for a good cause. We decided to expand our initiative, to involve more kids, even adults if they want to help. We're going to call this movement '*LIVE FOR LEAVES.*' At least we can do something for our land, for our planet Earth. We failed in our first project, but now we are more determined to continue our goal," said Arl.

He didn't mind telling their new friend all that. There was nothing to be ashamed of.

"Yes," said Angika. "We lost this battle, but we won our determination. I just thought of writing a song with that theme."

"Yes, that's a good idea, but you're going to sing it. Don't count me in on this one," said Zeke.

"You are winners," said Anzear, "You did a cold job. Awesome. The planet should be proud of you."

"You mean a *cool* job," said Zeke. "All this time we got confused when you said *cold*. Actually, you meant *cool*."

Talking and walking, the friends got close to the fence. "Nothing is missing," said Arl, checking the tools inside. He and Zeke started to fix the broken part of the fence. Angika was pulling the materials out of the circular fence. Anzear was paying close attention to everything they were doing. They finished with the fence, grabbed their buckets, and Arl asked the others if they wanted to grab a snack or something.

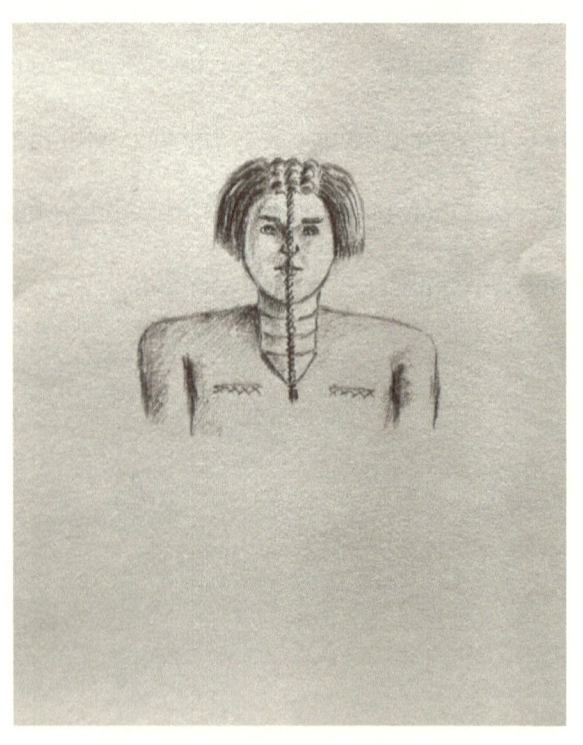

CHAPTER 10

Zeke unleashed Pepe and both started to walk toward the lake. When the lake appeared, Pepe started to run hastily. He loved playing with water.

"Beautiful," said Anzear. Pepe ran like a bullet straight to the lake. He never stopped barking. Anzear followed him. First he put his forefinger in the water, waited for a few seconds, and then walked into the lake with his clothes on. The kids opened their eyes as wide as a Ping-Pong ball. They looked at each other as if they wanted to say, 'Is this guy crazy or what?' Anzear was making all kinds of strange movements. He disappeared inside the lake for a few seconds. Then he got out of the lake, and to their amazement, he was as dry as he could be. "That was really interesting," said Anzear with a big smile. "We should get this in our town. Liquid that doesn't taste; changes its form, and is not poisoned. Awesome!"

The friends didn't know what to say. This foreigner was really strange. Maybe he was a magician.

They just had to wait and see if there were more surprises.

"Do you want an apple?" asked Angika Anzear, as she was looking in her backpack.

"Yes," said Anzear, very excitedly. "This is cold," continued Anzear looking at the apple. Then he saw the kids looking at him. "This is cool, yes."

"Oh, okay," said the kids at the same time.

"You can eat it. These are fresh from the farm," said Angika, taking a big bite from her apple.

"Farm!" Anzear took a last look at his apple and shoved the whole thing into his mouth. The apple disappeared into his body. "Interesting," said Anzear, very relaxed.

"What did you do? You're going to choke. Oh my goodness! Drink some water," said frightened

Angika. She handed him a bottle of water. Anzear took the bottle, staring at it from top to bottom.

"Water inside the bottle! Water outside the bottle!" said Anzear, pointing to the lake. "Awesome!" And he shoved the whole bottle in his mouth without blinking an eye. Angika backed up, really scared. She looked at Arl and Zeke. Their faces were like they had just seen a ghost. Actually, this was scarier than a ghost. This was *real*.

"Are you a magician? I am sure you are," insisted Angika.

"You have to tell us more about yourself, buddy. We told you enough. No more playing around, please," Arl said firmly.

"Yes," said Zeke. "You're acting very strangely. Foreigners are a little different, but we eat and drink in the same way. We save the plastic bottles for recycle. Where did you put yours? What kind of tricks did you use?"

"Magician, tricks, recycles. Why are you kids not happy? I don't understand," said Anzear.

"You are hiding something, definitely," said Arl. "We need an answer if you want to be our friend."

"What is up, pals?" Anzear paused for a while. Then he answered. "Yes, I want to be your friend. You are good creatures."

"Creatures?" said Angika frustrated. "We are people, humans and good ones."

"I understand now," said Anzear. "It is time to get back to my town. I will explain everything. That's why I came here, to convince myself that you are really good *creatures*, I mean good people. I am sorry for the disturbance. My name is not Anzear. I don't know how to pronounce it in your language. It's close to Sirus.

"Let's start somewhere else. Come with me. I want to show you something." The kids hesitated a bit, looked at each other, then followed Anzear or Sirus as he called himself. They stayed a few feet behind. Zeke tightened Pepe's leash in his hand and pulled him closer. Anzear was walking in the direction of the forest, followed by Arl, Angika, Zeke and Pepe.

Everything that moved in the forest caught Anzear's attention. They kept walking and stopping because of Anzear. Finally he stopped at the *trees with five leaves.* He looked up in the sky, and then made a sign with his hands, creating a rhombus. The kids looked int the sky, too. There was nothing. They looked at each other for an answer to this trick, and then looked at

Anzear again. He got close to one of the three trees. Suddenly, Pepe started to bark, looking in one direction. The kids looked in that direction and they saw another dog, standing more than a hundred feet away, staring at them. They couldn't determine what kind of a dog he was, except it looked white. From that distance, it seemed more like a ghost. After a few seconds, Pepe ran like a bullet toward this 'white ghost', a dog that appeared from nowhere. Maybe he thought he had found a friend.

"Pepe! Stop!" shouted Zeke, and he ran after him. Pepe was too fast for Zeke. As Pepe got closer to the white dog, that dog didn't move an inch. It stood like a statue. Then the statue disappeared.

"What happened? Did he hide behind a bush or something?" asked Angika. Arl just stood there, unable to talk. Anzear was looking around, making 360 degrees motion with his head.

"Let's go check it out," said Arl, shaking his head as if he had awakened from a dream. He ran in the same direction Zeke ran, followed by Angika. Anzear was walking toward them slowly. He was still looking around and sometimes looking up in the sky. Zeke kept running, but couldn't get closer to Pepe.

"Pepe, come here, buddy," said Zeke. Pepe barked at Zeke once and ran behind a bush, like he wanted to play 'hide and seek.' "Where did you go? It's not time to play now," said Zeke, looking behind the bush.

"Where is the white dog?" asked Angika.

"Where is Pepe?" asked Arl.

"There was no white dog," said Zeke. "But now I can't find Pepe." He was checking behind every tree close by. Then he pulled a treat from his right pocket and raised his right hand. "Here buddy, I've got something for you." There was no response.

A few feet behind, Anzear made a rhombus sign again, with his arms stretched toward the sky. Then he approached the three friends. A quiet bark could be heard. It seemed like it was from far away. Kids were checking around to see if they could find Pepe. Then, they heard the bark again. This time it was louder, but not up close. It seemed like the wind brought it to them.

"It seems like the bark is in the air," said Arl. "Wait a minute." Arl was trying to listen with one hand behind his right ear. "The sound comes from above," continued Arl. They turned their heads up. The barking got louder. The kids were looking up, on the trees, between the branches and leaves. They were trying to find where the bark was coming from.

"I think I saw Pepe," said Angika, pointing up to a poplar tree.

"Yes, it is Pepe," said Arl. "How did he get up there? I can't believe it."

"How, on Earth, did he climb up there?" asked Zeke. "He never did that before. Then again, what kind of dog can do that? Now, what am I going to do? We're too far from the city and firefighters."

"That's really strange. We're going to come up with something, Zeke," said Arl scratching his head. He paused for a bit. "How about if we make a T-shirt bed so Pepe can jump and we catch him," continued Arl with eyes wide open.

"That's a good idea," said Angika. "We can gather some branches with leaves and make a big pile, just in case Pepe misses the shirts. What do you think, Zeke?

"It sounds good. The only thing I wonder is who's going to convince Pepe to jump? He looks pretty scared. I don't blame him." Then Arl started to take his shirt off. "Let's try it anyway." Angika, who was wearing a tank top under her T-shirt, followed Arl. They tied their shirts together.

"It's not a big bed," said Arl. "Let's make the bed with branches and leaves like Angika said. "They walked around to collect tiny branches. After each one got a handful, they made a pile. Then, they grabbed the T-shirt bed with both hands, while creating a circle. Arl said:

"Ready?"

"Ready," said Angika and Zeke at the same time.

"You call him, Zeke. Pepe listens to you better than to anyone," said Arl.   "Ok…Pepe, Pepe, here buddy. I already miss you."

"Come, Pepe, jump," Arl and Angika started to call him. They could hear Pepe barking and whining every now and then.

"It's not working," said Zeke. "Maybe I will have to climb all the way up there. But how?"

"You come and step on my shoulders," said Arl. "That's going to give you a better reach. Let's try it."

"I don't know," said Zeke. "That tree is too tall, even like that."

"Like the game 'horseman,'" said Arl as he squatted by the tree trunk. Zeke took his sneakers off.

Then he put his left foot on Arl's left shoulder and after that, the right one on the right shoulder. He was hugging the tree to keep his balance. Arl got up slowly. Zeke tried to reach the first big branch, but couldn't. They missed by just one foot.

"Darn it," said Zeke.

"Maybe I can reach it. I am a little taller," said Angika.

"And a lot lighter," said Arl, trying to bring a little humor into the situation.

"May I help? I can help," said Anzear.

The kids turned their heads toward Anzear as though they were seeing him for the first time. They totally forgot that he was there.

"Yes, you are a lot taller. I don't know whether or not you are heavier," said Arl.

"I am not going up there. Pepe is going to come down here," said Anzear as he was backing up.

"I think we know that Pepe has to come down here," said Zeke. "But how? He is afraid to jump. I don't blame him for that. And certainly dogs don't know how to fly, either. So, what's your great sug…?" Suddenly, Zeke's jaw just dropped and he just stood there with his mouth open. His eyes got bigger than his mouth as he was looking up.

Angika covered her mouth with her left hand like she was trying to keep her jaw from not dropping down. Arl was another living statue. All this happened because Pepe was really flying down in slow motion. He was very quiet, sometimes just blinking his eyes.

The first one to move was Zeke. He tried to get in a good position, so he could catch Pepe. He walked unconsciously those few steps, like he was sleepwalking. Then Arl turned around and saw Anzear. Anzear's eyes were fixed. His arms were straight out with his palms facing up toward Pepe. Arl was looking at Pepe and sometimes at Anzear. As Anzear's arms were going down slowly, so was Pepe. Pepe finally jumped right into Zeke's arms. As soon as he made contact with Zeke, Pepe started to lick Zeke's face all over. Arl and Angika walked over to Zeke and started to pat Pepe.

"You hairy boy. You scared us to death," said Angika in a vibrating voice.

"Good job, Pepe. You were very brave," said Arl. "But we really should thank Anzear."

"Thanks buddy. I really appreciate it. I didn't know how we were going to help him, far away from the city," said Zeke as he was untying his shirt from the others thrown on the ground earlier.

"Something is not right," said Anzear. "Pepe going up like that? I have to do something."

"I don't think you should do such a horrible thing to an innocent creature," said Arl. "And don't say we did it. The only thing we can do is build a kite, not make dogs fly."

"Horrible?" Anzear paused for a few seconds. "Horrible is too bad. We have good intentions."

"Who is 'we'" asked Angika.

"Everything should be under control. Something is malfunctioning. I am going to find out really soon." Anzear lifted his right arm to his chest level. A square light popped up, then turned into a screen. Arl approached and looked at it, but couldn't make any sense of the signs that he saw. He looked at Anzear for an explanation.

"I notice that …" Anzear stopped. He backed up one step. The screen went back to his arm. A cylinder look-alike popped up from his right leg. He aimed it at the three friends.

Arl moved in front of Angika. "Sit down," he said. Zeke covered Pepe and wanted to sit down, too, but he couldn't. A transparent balloon covered all of them.

"What is this?" asked Angika. "Let's get out of here."

"We can't. We're trapped. He tricked us," said Zeke.

"How could he?" declared Angika. "I can't believe we were so naive."

"Wait," said Arl. "I think something else is involved."

Anzear was looking around. Often he looked up. Suddenly a bright light, like a fire, surrounded him. He started to wander around, always surrounded by the circle of light.

"You are safe. Be patient," said Anzear to the kids.

Arl started to hear some strange sounds coming from nowhere. Then he noticed Anzear making some weird sounds, too.

"Is he talking?" asked Angika.

"Maybe. Who knows?" said Arl.

An arrow of fire flashed toward Anzear from inside the trees.

"Look! He's changing his clothes," said Angika.

"He's changing the whole body, but it is getting too blurry to see clearly," said Arl, trying to get a better view. Pepe kept barking and barking and trying to bite the balloon.

"Sorry, I can't stop him," said Zeke. "Now it is getting darker too. A blue arrow is coming toward us," continued Zeke, while he was covering Pepe. Arl covered Angika as they squatted.

"We are hiding like ostriches in the sand," said Arl.

"Nice time for a joke," said Angika.

"No. I meant we should do something. Maybe we can make the balloon roll or something. I've seen it on TV. Some people do that for fun. What am I saying? There's only one person in the balloon when they do that.

We are four. We are going to be like mashed potatoes in the end," Arl said, sounding desperate.

"Gosh! We can't see anything now. It became like night without the moon," said Zeke.

"I don't think we are touching the ground. Do you?" asked Arl.

"No. I think we're flying," said Angika.

"Let's hold each othe…." Arl couldn't finish his sentence. His mouth suddenly would not move as though it were frozen shut. The same happened with his eyes and his arms when he tried to reach Angika. Angika got frozen, too, trying to keep her balance. It seemed like she was trying to say something: something that started with an O. Her hair was waving in the air on the right side. On the other side, Zeke bent his knees, holding Pepe in his arms. He got frozen, too. His eyes were wide open. His eyebrows created a V shape. Pepe was also frozen, with his eyes looking at Zeke. His tongue was hanging on the left side of his open mouth. Altogether, they looked like an old painting, hanging on the wall of an art museum. The only difference was that they wore modern clothes and they were three-dimensional.

CHAPTER 11

The first one to break the silence was Pepe. He barked twice and started to lick Zeke as though he hadn't seen him for days. Then, one by one, the people in the painting were coming to life.

"Oh, buddy, you're okay!" said Zeke, sounding very relieved.

"What happened? Where are we? It is light inside, but it's still dark outside the balloon," said Angika, looking around.

"We just have to wait and see. There are a lot of unanswered questions. We will wait and see with our eyes open, no longer frozen shut. This force is very powerful. It even can open and close our eyes whenever it wants to," said Arl.

"Only Anzear can be a match for this mysterious force or creature," said Angika. "And we don't even know what happened to him after all." She sat down.

Zeke asked Pepe to sit, and then he sat down, too. Then he stood on his fists. "We can touch the ground. We totally forgot," said Zeke.

Arl jumped once like he was on a trampoline. "The ground is very hard, like a stone. The balloon is very soft, but unbreakable. The ground doesn't feel like a river stone, though. It's kind of flat. I can't believe it got dark so fast," said Arl. "Where does the light inside come from? I have no idea. It feels like I am having a bad dream. But the worst part is that I'm sharing it with you."

"We shared everything together," said Zeke. "And most of it is good memories."

"Why do you say that?" asked Angika. "It was you who carried me when I fell off my bike? Right in front of the bus?"

"Was that in the 4th grade?" asked Arl, with a smile. "I couldn't carry you any longer and we both fell right on the edge of the sidewalk and on the grass."

"The bus driver started to yell at us when he saw that we were okay. We deserved that," said Angika.

Pepe saw the kids laughing and started to bark, wagging his tail left and right.

"I think Pepe is trying to tell his troublemaking story, too," said Zeke. "He has plenty of those, mostly with cats. But the most frightening one is the story about the lady in the wheelchair. She was looking for her cat, a brown grayish cat. She was calling the cat. I think his name was Ripley. Pepe was watching everything. I was walking him down the street when he suddenly started to run like crazy toward the cat. I don't know, maybe he wanted to stop the cat from running. I couldn't hang onto the leash, so it went flying into the air, left and right. At some point, the leash got tangled in one of the wheels of the wheelchair and started to pull the wheelchair as he was running. The road was downhill. The old lady got confused. She lost control of the wheelchair. The wheelchair became a dog chariot. I tried to catch up with them, but the wheels and paws were faster than I was."

"Then Arl and I showed up with our bikes. The cat jumped into the basket, in front of my bike," recalled Angika.

"Pepe jumped on me, happy to see me," said Arl. "The old lady almost fell backward. By that time, you came and held onto the arms of the wheelchair so it would stop moving down the hill."

"You could see the tears in her eyes. Either from joy or horror," said Angika.

"Joy and horror. Sounds like our story today," said Zeke. He grabbed Pepe and held him tight.

Arl looked at them. Angika did not show any emotion, but Arl felt like she could burst into tears any second. "We're going to stick together and everything will be okay. This must be a bad joke after all," said Arl.

"I wonder what happened to Anzear," said Angika. "Did he get hurt from that last blast?"

"Here I am. I am okay." A hoarse voice came from really nearby. A few beeps followed that voice. Then a different voice followed: "Anzear is here." Slowly the light was pushing away the darkness. In a few seconds, the darkness was gone. Arl noticed that the balloon was gone, too. A few feet away stood a strange looking creature. Was this creature supposed to be Anzear? they wondered.

CHAPTER 12

Don't you think this is a sick joke, Anzear?" said Arl, looking at him from top to bottom. All he could see was hair all over his body, even on his face.

"What happened to your voice? Why did you change your appearance?" asked Angika.

Pepe backed up "Relax, buddy. He's not going to harm you. What's with the hair?" asked Zeke. "Are you going to compete with Pepe?"

"Changed appearance. Different voice. Hair like a dog's hair. Complicated. I am Anzear. We met outside. It is I, Anzear. One and the same." He started to check himself, left, right, up, down. The kids were looking at each other. When Anzear turned his back, trying to figure out what was wrong with his appearance, something was hanging on the back of his neck. Then, that thing moved.

Angika got close to Arl and whispered in his ear; "Don't you think that's creepy?

"Is that a …?" Arl didn't finish his sentence. He started to look at Pepe.

"A tail?" said Zeke and Arl at the same time.

Anzear turned his head. "Tail? Animal? Human… no tail. Wings? No wings." He looked at Pepe, then at the kids. "Yes. No, no tail. Where is your hair my friends?"

"Is he still playing with us? I've got enough of him," said Zeke in low voice.

"Let's wait a little longer," said Arl. "I know something is not right. He seemed cooler earlier. Let's just keep an eye on him all the time. Hair? We just shaved yesterday," said Arl, joking. "As far as tail, it is not in style anymore. Right, Angika? You're the expert on this."

"Who, me? Oh, yes. Expert. No. No tail. No fur, either." She looked at Arl "Am I making any sense?" Arl made a sign meaning "go ahead," and continued. "Yes, we are using fur less and less. But the tail? We stopped that for good. We left the tail and hair to some animals. We've got the other stuff."

"Stuff?" asked Zeke. Angika raised her shoulders.

"No hair. No tail. We can fix that. I love the tail." Anzear paused. "I love the animals, birds, insects, and dinosaurs. Where can I find a dinosaur? They are so big and powerful."

"If you want to see them, go to the museum," said Angika. "There are no dinosaurs in our forest."

"I noticed that. What did you do to them?" asked Anzear. "Eliminate them, so you can take over?"

"We don't know for sure what happened to them. If you want to know more, go to the Museum of Natural History or to the library. "We didn't take over anything. You took us over. First, you acted like a good guy, now you are asking questions. Tell us! Where are we? No more playing around," said Arl, looking around for an exit.

Then Angika took over. "Dinosaurs are believed to have been on Earth millions of years ago. There wasn't any sign of humans at that time." She looked at Arl. Arl looked back at her.

"Keep talking," he motioned soundlessly with his lips. Arl was still trying to find a clue as to where they were. All he could see was a stone wall and a stone floor.

It seemed like they were inside a boulder. Arl was thinking, *how did we get here? It's freaking me out. How we are going to get out of here is even more challenging.* His vision was blurry, but he thought he saw a hallway on his right side. Anzear was in front, Angika on his left, and on the far left, Zeke with Pepe. Arl slowly took a step back. With his left hand, he tried to move Angika in front of him. She kept talking about dinosaurs. *Good, she didn't miss any of those classes,* Arl was thinking as he took another step back.

"Do you want to be in the bubble again, my friend? Or do you like being a living sculpture better?" That was Anzear, holding a cylinder look-alike toy in his hand. That was the same thing he had pulled out from the pocket of his unusual pants earlier.

"But where did he keep that now that he had changed his appearance?" wondered Arl. Anzear turned his back. Then suddenly, everything turned dark.

"Nobody moves! Is that clear, my friends?" asked Anzear.

CHAPTER 13

The light came back on. Then he turned again. "Are you happy now? I've got nice clothes. You call them nice. No more tail, no hair. Still some? How about now?" His head turned shiny like a glass bowl. "Still not cool? How about a cap? Let us put it on backwards." He raised his left arm in front of his chest. A screen popped out again. Different symbols and pictures were moving at lightning speed. Dozens of different hats and shapes were changing on Anzear's head. "Maybe I should wear it to the side? Or is this one better? "Do you like the police hat or the astronaut one? You don't deserve that. Let us stick with no hat." Now he looked like a shiny manikin. Again, the shoes, pants and jacket were one piece, now in dark grayish color. The neck was very round, almost like a pipe. And the pipe neck was connected to this perfectly shaped head. The eye color changed regularly. There was not a single piece of hair on the eyelashes, nor on the eyebrows.

Arl still had his right foot pointed in the right direction. He was thinking, *there's something we must do, but we're no match against his powers. Let's see what he's up to.*

"I was just curious. What kind of rocks are these? I love rocks. I am very interested in them," said Arl in a loud voice.

"I thought you love cement on this planet. You like to blow rocks. A little power you've got and you destroy things. That is going to stop," said Anzear. "With your help, too."

"We'd like to help," said Zeke, "but first tell us where we are. Who are you? Where did you come from?"

"First, do not forget the bubble," said Anzear. "Second, you can help by giving your dog to me."

"No way. Over my dead body," said Zeke, pushing his chest forward.

Anzear didn't move an inch. "I want you alive and healthy. That is what my superiors want, anyway. They are so weak." Anzear paused briefly and then he continued. "I need two dogs. I already have one. So your hairy dog will make a couple."

"What are you going to do to them?" asked Angika, stepping in front of Zeke. "You want to learn about dogs? We can help you with that."

"I want to learn how to make the dogs fight. Fight like a dog. Dogfights." said Anzear.

"How can we convince you?" asked Arl.

"You don't have to. I am going to find out for myself, after I have everything I need. That's why I am here. To do the right thing," said Anzear.

"Earlier, you said that you are going to show us something. We're waiting," said Arl.

"That was totally naive of Anzear, to say. That's why I showed up," said Anzear.

"Wait a minute," said Angika. "You said it and then you thought it was naive. And then you showed up. What showed up? The tail? Or the hair on your face?"

Anzear's eyes got smaller, and then became a normal size again. "Your tone does not sound normal, my friend. What do you know female species? Except makeup, hairdo's, nails? Oh, you know music. You call it music. To me, it is screaming for help. You know nothing about the real world. Maybe I have to show you. Actually, I need a couple of your species, too. The species that is destroying the habitat," finished Anzear.

"Take me," said Arl, seeing that the conversation was going the wrong way.

"Okay. But I need the female, too" said Anzear. "And the lovely dog."

Zeke looked at Pepe. Then he swatted down beside him. He got up again and put his hand in his right pocket. He pulled out a couple of treats and through them in the direction where Arl had wanted to go earlier. And that was to his right. "Run, Pepe, run!" yelled Zeke. Pepe started to run. Zeke followed him, but they couldn't go very far. Anzear used his "toy" and froze them so they couldn't move. Another sound came from his "toy" and he put both of them into a balloon that he liked to call a "bubble." Then Angika ran in the other direction, toward Anzear, without knowing where. She couldn't take three steps. She ended up in another balloon, like Zeke and Pepe. Arl took his chances and ran in Zeke's direction. He made it to the hallway, but it was dark there. He kept hitting walls time after time. After a few wall crashes, Arl noticed a dim light. He continued moving toward that light, looking back continually. As he got closer, the light was taking a round shape. The light didn't get brighter, but the round shape multiplied.

    'Multiple balloons? Where am I? What's going on? What are these things inside the balloons? Toys?' Arl wondered. Then he saw a couple of peacocks inside one of the balloons, then, a couple of cats, a couple of squirrels, and a couple of wolves. The birds and the animals were normal sized and had normal looking bodies. Their eyes were open. Some of them had their mouths open, too. Every balloon was big enough for each couple to fit into. Then Arl saw balloons with insects and worms. "This looks like an animal, bird and insect museum," said Arl while walking around the balloons. He heard something. That reminded him that Anzear was after him. He turned around quickly and then he saw another hallway. Arl ran fast in that direction. No lights again. He stretched his arms out to the side and walked like a blind person, to avoid bumping into the walls. The hallway wasn't that long. Arl took almost twenty steps, going slightly to the left. In the end, he noticed the circle lights again. "Balloons again? If this is a museum, why is it kept dark? Where is the entrance?

Where is the exit? Most of all, what is Anzear doing

here?" With these questions in mind, Arl got very close

to the balloons. This time, inside them, Arl saw all

different kinds of flowers. Then he saw some filled with

acorns. *Anzear might be here any second,* he thought.

Those ones look like seeds. Those must be roots. Another

section was filled with balloons that had fruits. Some of

them Arl recognized and others he had never seen before.

Moving around, Arl got to the vegetable section. This

section was different from the others. This one had 3-

dimensional photos of people planting seeds, watering,

harvesting, carrying them by hand or auto, eating them.

"Grandpa Toke.!" Arl was stunned when he saw GT's

photo, working on their garden. It was a photo taken

from the air. GT had never mentioned somebody taking a

photo of him. *Maybe he forgot,* thought Arl. "But, why

was there a boulder in the dark? Was it a warehouse?" Whatever it was, Arl felt that he had to find out. "I have to do something for my friends," he said to himself. "I need to get out of here, to get help. I can't believe Anzear turned out to be such a jerk. Actually a dangerous jerk." Arl kept looking left and right. Some empty balloons caught his attention. Next to them were pictures of oceans, lakes, rivers, streams, creeks, waterfalls, and deserts. "This must be the water section," he said, "but there is no sign of water creatures. No sign of water fauna."

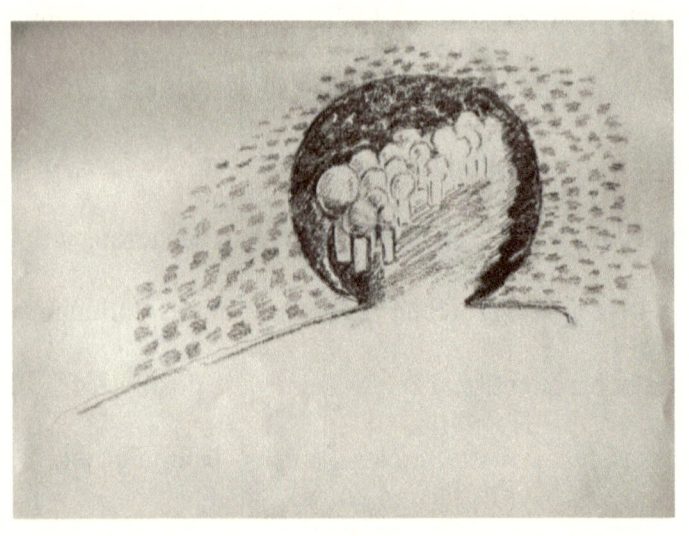

CHAPTER 14

"Do you like my collection?" Anzear broke the silence. "It is not complete yet. You are going to help me, starting with the lake and its mysteries. This time, you and your friends are going to be on our side." Anzear was moving slowly toward Arl. Arl was walking backwards, looking at both sides to prevent crashing into any balloons. There was not much room to move. There was not much time to think. *How can I beat this monster?* Arl was wondering. *There must be a way to stop him. There must be a weak spot.* With these things in mind, Arl tried to run, but something sharp hit his left thigh. He looked at Anzear holding his "toy," ready for another shot. Then he looked at his leg. There was no blood or any sign of an opening. A burning sensation spread throughout his leg, though. Arl tried to move again, but the pain made him scream very loud. A couple of balloons nearby disappeared.

"You coward!" screamed Arl on top of his lungs. Another balloon vanished. Arl was observing everything around him as he was screaming. He decided to give it another try. "You backstabber!" This time, he screamed as loud as he possibly could. Another two balloons vanished. *Wow, I could never thought of that. Let's hope he doesn't notice, Arl was thinking.*

Anzear was looking at the screen that he had checked earlier. "Coward, backstabber. Coward, I cannot accept. But, backstabber is not being clarified yet. I can say that I am a front-stabber, side-stabber, too, if I want to. You want me to demonstrate it?"

"No. I know your powers already,"Arl said quickly. "I like your collection, by the way. I am trying to build a collection of rocks. But nothing compared to yours. I want to get a couple of rocks from this boulder, too. Is that okay?" asked Arl with a half smile.

"You can collect them anytime. This boulder is not going anywhere. My collection is coming with me. Hopefully, you too. But first we have to finish my small collection. You see? I am missing my liquid room. This is the most important part of my collection. So together, we are going to start from the lake," said Anzear, who didn't put his "toy" back in place. The screen was gone. Let us walk. I'll follow you, or if you like, you can follow me in the bubble," continued Anzear.

I hate it when he says "bubble," thought Arl. "I can walk. See?" said Arl, who noticed that the pain was gone.

"So, I am a coward and backscratcher?" asked Anzear.

"Not at all. But, when we get scared, we say stuff we don't always mean what we say," explained Arl.

"We don't say anything. We just freeze," said Anzear.

"So basically, you shut up," said Arl.

Anzear paused for a few seconds "No. We shut everything up and down until we adjust to the situation."

"Yes, that's what I meant," said Arl, worrying that he might get frozen, too. That reminded him of Zeke and Angika. "We're going to need some help, too. My friends are very good swimmers. Pepe too," continued Arl.

"Very well. We can finish quicker like that. After you," said Anzear, pointing in the direction where he came from. Suddenly, everything got brighter. "You can see better now. That does not mean you can run better."

Arl started walking. Now he could see that they were inside a boulder, but he didn't stop for a more detailed view. Anzear was right after him and he didn't want any more complications. The boulder didn't seem natural. It was too perfect. The walls looked like a dozen sculptors had chiseled them. There wasn't any light bulb or a light switch. No signs, no directions. The rooms were separated by walls and connected by hallways. There were no doors. Basically, it was just stonewalls and the balloons.

Who made that? That has to be found out later, when the time comes, thought Arl. Now that it was brighter, the distance seemed shorter for Arl. Soon they arrived in a round room with some chiseled walls. Still, there was no entrance, and no doors. The only things Arl could see were the big balloons, with Zeke, Angika and Pepe inside them. Anzear pulled his "toy" out pointing it at them, and in a blink of an eye, the balloons were gone. "Angika, Zeke, Pepe! Are you okay?" Arl worriedly asked.

"Angika, Arl! Oh, you are okay," said Zeke after he held Pepe in his arms. They all hugged and looked at each other.

"What is this? opening your arms around each other?" asked Anzear. "Oh, I see," he said, after looking at the screen in front of him. "Can you give me a hug too?" asked Anzear, with his arms open.

"You backstabber! Don't come any closer," said Zeke, pointing his left forefinger at him.

"What is it with you using the word 'backscratcher'?" asked Anzear. "All I did was put you inside a bubble. And I can do that in any position: front, back, and side."

"It's okay Zeke. All he wants is to help him with his collection. We misunderstood the whole thing," intervened Arl, looking Zeke straight in the eye. "We thought," Continued Arl, turning his head toward Angika, "that a war started or something. But in reality, all Anzear wanted was to build a collection. I am collecting stones. He wants to build a bigger collection, with more varieties. Do you want to show them Anzear?" concluded Arl.

"Why not? I have nothing to hide from you. You are part of my collection anyway." Anzear paused. Then he said, "I wanted to say, you will have your part in building my collection. Let me show you. Arl, you can lead the way."

"Wow. This is like a tunnel and these are real rocks," said Angika as she touched the side of the hallway.

"And these are perfectly carved," said Zeke. "Who made this? And why?"

"That is not important right now. You do as I say and the Earth will be fine. You will be fine. Actually, much better," said Anzear.

"You are…" started Zeke, but Arl intervened again.

"You are going to be amazed, Zeke. Wait and see. Just wait," said Arl, looking at Zeke again straight in the eye. "You're going to love the flower collection, Angika. It's out of this world."

"Actually, everything needs to be out of *this* world. We are going to make your world a better one," said Anzear.

"But..," Angika started and then stopped with her mouth open. First room appeared. "I never saw this many creatures in one place. And they look like they're going to move any second," finished Angika in louder voice, like she wanted to wake them up.

"They are not going to move for a long time. So relax," said Anzear.

Pepe started to bark. "How can we relax with all these dead animals? Did you see these, Arl?" asked Zeke, holding Pepe tighter.

"They are not dead. They are asleep. You see this dog? He needs a friend. And he is not a "hot dog" yet. Everything is in couples, if they come that way," explained Anzear. Zeke moved a step toward Anzear, but Arl pulled him back and almost tore his shirt.

"They can't breathe inside these balloons. How can they survive?" asked Angika.

"You are timeless behind in our galaxy, my friend. We are going to fix that. For me, these creatures are far safer like this than outside in the wild, with predators like you," responded Anzear.

Angika looked at Arl and Zeke. Arl could see the frustration in her eyes.

"They are alive," said Arl, remembering how they got frozen, too, for a while. "It's like they got frozen in time. Let's check the other rooms." Arl walked into the hallway that led to what was called "the green room."

They walked in silence. Angika approached Arl and whispered," I don't want to see more dead things. Let's get out of here!"

"How?" asked Arl. "Just be patient. I have a plan. Tell Zeke, too. Look at all this greenery. Isn't our planet beautiful?"

"It used to be better," intervened Anzear. "Maybe you got tired of it. Maybe you do not want it anymore. Maybe the planet does not want you anymore"

"Look," said Angika, pointing at GT's photo.

"I know," said Arl. "I don't know what to tell you. Let's finish here quickly and go into the other room, "the liquid room," Arl said in a louder voice. "Anzear needs our help to finish faster. He can tell us more."

"I am going to fill the empty bubbles with as many water creatures as I can. You are going to help me with the lake, your lovely lake. And this is just the beginning. You have a lot of water on your planet. Actually, you have more than you deserve and need. I will take care of the bubbles. You are going to take care of the lake part. You can show your swimming abilities. Okay, my friends?" questioned Anzear.

"We are not..," yelled Zeke. Then he thought better of it, looked at Arl, and quickly said to Anzear, "going to let you down." Arl nodded his head in agreement.

"Let me down?" repeated Anzear. "Well, you are going down to the lake. I am going to help you from outside the lake."

"Okay. Let's do that," said Arl, trying not to waste time with the word "play." "After you Anzear."

Everything turned dark again. After a couple of seconds, the light came back on and the kids found themselves inside the balloon again. But this time, Pepe was missing. So was Anzear!

"Pepe, Pepe! What did he do to him?" asked Zeke very worried. "How are we going to find him?"

"We're going to find a way. Just stay calm. Let me show you my plan," said Arl. "I noticed earlier that when I screamed, a couple of balloons popped up. Well, they didn't really pop up, but they disappeared. The balloon that we are standing in right now is bigger. But, if we all scream together at the same time, we might crack this one, too. What do you think, buddies?"

"We've got nothing to lose," said Zeke.

"When are we going to know that it is the right time for screaming?" asked Angika as she started to clear the throat.

"I guess a good idea is to be far from Anzear and close to a place where we can hide. We already know his powers. Meanwhile, we'll look for a better option. Okay? Here, "3 G's," said Arl, stretching his arm.

Angika followed with a smile: "3G's."

"3G's", echoed Zeke. "Now or never. It's time for action. We're not going to let this creep push us around."

"Let's remain calm if we can. We can think better like that," said Arl. "Let's take a deep breath, just like the physical education teacher tells us to do."

"Looks like you're having fun. What is that, some kind of a dance?" asked Anzear. The kids looked at him without moving a muscle.

"So, we're here by the lake," whispered Zeke. "Why does he need us here? He didn't need anybody before."

"I remember when he went in the water earlier. He didn't even get wet," said Angika. He was very excited, too. Why is he scared now?"

"A lot of things have changed since that arrow of fire hit him from inside the forest. Maybe he lost some of his powers," said Arl. "We're going to find out pretty soon. Let's act normal. Well, kind of normal under these circumstances."

"It is time for you humans to return a favor to the lake," said Anzear. The balloon with the three friends inside went inside the water slowly and started to move to the surface of the lake.

"You're not coming with us?" asked Arl.

"No, I prefer no liquid," said Anzear.

The kids looked at each other. Anzear pulled another cylinder look- alike from his invisible pocket and inserted it into the water. After a few seconds, he pulled it out of the water. Countless sparkles filled the surface of the water about twenty feet from shore. The sparkles lasted for sixty seconds. Then they were replaced with white bellies of fish that were coming to surface.

"Not too many," said Anzear. "There are supposed to be a lot more. Another sign of the bad behavior of humans. It is time to save what is left. Get to work," ordered Anzear as he threw three bowls on top of the surface. The bowls, which looked like they were made of glass, were bigger than a basketball, with two holes in each one. They were floating on the water, as the balloon with the three friends was static in the air, about thirty feet away.

"If we scream now, can we make it to the other side?" asked Zeke.

"We might, but is too dangerous," said Arl.

"Then again, he's going to wait for us on other side," said Angika. "We have to think, think and think!"

"How about if we can make him come inside the water and then we go from there?" suggested Zeke.

"Not a bad idea," said Arl. "Let's try it before he makes us go in the water. Listen, Anzear, the further we go into the lake, the more species we'll find. That's because the water gets very deep. That's where the monster's home is."

"Monsters? I like monsters. OK, I will make you go further. I will give you this toy to use," and he was reaching down to his right leg.

"Why don't you come with us?" said Arl. "We can do a much better job with you advising us."

"I am sure of that. You understand it, too. Let us ride in the bubble then. But you will do the swimming."

Inside the bubble, slowly Arl, Angika and Zeke were flying toward the shore.

"When I say now, we all are going to start screaming on top of our lungs," said Arl.

"We'll wait for a distance that we think we can handle swimming," said Zeke.

"Done," said Angika.

"Done," repeated Arl.

As soon as they arrived on the shore, everything turned black. A few seconds went by and the kids found themselves in a bigger balloon. For the first time, they had Anzear that close. Arl tried to look indifferent. He gradually tried to move closer to Anzear, but something unexplainable was pushing him away. Something invisible.

"You don't seem comfortable. I can help you." Anzear quickly pointed his "toy" toward Arl and something like a laser went through the three friends.

Arl looked at Angika. She looked back at him. Then Arl noticed that he couldn't move his arms or his legs. *Here we go again,* thought Arl. The only thing he could move was his head. He could see the frustration in Zeke's eyes. The balloon was going faster toward the middle of the lake, this time higher than before. Arl couldn't enjoy the beauty of the lake from the sky under those circumstances. They got about one hundred and fifty feet from shore. Arl looked at Zeke, then at Angika.

"Ready to sing buddies? Now!" said Arl. All three friends started to scream as hard as they could. Zeke's voice was the strongest. His eyes looked like they were going to pop out. Angika's face was getting very red.

"What are you doing? Are you scared or are you three losing your minds?" asked Anzear. Before he finished the sentence, the balloon disappeared and they all fell into the lake. One by one, they were coming up to the surface: Arl, Zeke and a few feet away, Angika.

"You swam under water? Very smart," said Zeke.

"Lucky we can move, too. Obviously, some of his powers don't work under the water," said Arl. "No sign of Anzear, either. Hurry up! I always wanted to race you Angika," continued Arl, as he quickly swam away.

"Not today, Arl. I'll give you another chance," said Angika as she swam away like a mermaid

Arl kept looking back for a sign of Anzear. No sign of him.

"Hurry up, buddies. The faster we go, the more chance we will have to do something," said Arl.

"We're getting close," said Zeke. "Look at those fish by the shore. They're moving."

"They're going to die," said Angika. "We have to throw them back in the water."

"I'll do that. You and Zeke go find that boulder and look for an entrance or something," said Arl. "Pepe is waiting for you, Zeke."

"No," said Zeke. "We're in this together."

"I'll catch up with you. It's not going to take that long," said Arl as he turned his head one more time. He noticed a whirlpool in the water. Angika had reached the shore already. In a few seconds, Zeke arrived, too.

"Come on, Arl. Hurry up," said Zeke. "Why did you stop? What are you looking at?" Zeke looked in the same direction Arl was looking too. "Wow!" The whirlpool was getting bigger.

"Zeke, Angika, run! I think he's coming out." Arl started to swim the rest of the distance faster. Angika and Zeke started to run, too. Then Angika stopped.

"No," said Angika. "One for all, all for one. Let's just wait for Arl." They were between the forest and the lake. Arl, who had already reached the shore, was picking up the last fish, hoping they might survive. "Hurry, Arl. He might come any second," said Angika in a low voice.

CHAPTER 15

"Hello buddies! How are you?" A familiar voice came from inside the forest.

"Who said that?" asked Angika, backing up one step.

Zeke picked up a stone. "Come out wherever you are," he said.

"I am Anzear. I came here to help you. I am sorry I could not come sooner." said Anzear.

"Not as sorry as we are," said Angika, looking toward the forest for a sign of him. "How did he get here so fast? That's not a surprise anymore," she answered herself. Anzear came out in the open.

"Now you decided to change your appearance again? With the first look that you tricked us with? Well, the last look fits you better. The jerky look," said Zeke.

"I never changed my look," said Anzear. "At least not after I met you kids."

Zeke backed up two steps and looked at Arl. "You better stay there, Ar..." He couldn't finish the sentence. From the lake, a giant bubble was floating toward the shore. Zeke quickly turned his head toward Anzear.

"How can he be in both places at the same time?" asked Angika, looking left and right.

"You thought you got rid of me? Now that you asked for it, you are going to scream for real. You are going to scream for your life, but only the fish are going to hear you." said Anzear, who came from the lake. Then he pulled out his "toy" and pointed it toward Arl. Anzear who came from the forest pulled out his "toy," too, and pointed it toward Arl whom he shot him with a laser beam. Arl froze. Anzear from the lake shot him with another laser beam that circled Arl's body in a violet line and started to raise him up into the air, about twenty-feet high. Then he turned his body toward the lake. With his right arm pointing up toward Arl, he moved Arl about thirty feet way from the shore and then dropped him. Angika started to run toward the lake. Zeke followed her, too.

"Stop, kids! This is my duty to take care of once and for all. You are going to freeze one more time and this is going to be the last time. I'm sorry," said Anzear who came from the forest as he quickly pointed the gun toward Angika and Zeke. Again they found themselves inside a balloon. Then another balloon covered the first one. And then another third balloon covered the two. Three balloons circled friends. They couldn't move, but they could see and hear. Angika looked at the lake. There was not a sign of Arl. Her eyes were growing misty, and then a tear dropped. She looked at Zeke. His eyes were getting moist, too. They turned their head and saw both Anzears walking toward each other. Both were carrying their toy guns and pointing it at each other.

"Stop! This is over," declared Anzear from the forest or the first Anzear they met who was dressed in a fancy suit.

"No, you are wrong. Everybody is wrong about this planet. I have a better solution," said the mean Anzear, who didn't stop walking forward.

"Then I have to use the last tool," said the first Anzear. He looked up in the sky and made the rhomb sign again. That didn't stop mean Anzear. He started shooting laser beams at good Anzear. Good Anzear froze with his hands in the air. Then mean Anzear pointed his toy gun toward the forest and four shots started to turn the forest on fire. Angika and Zeke's eyes were coming out of their sockets. Angika closed her eyes. Zeke's eyes were turning red. Mean Anzear turned toward them.

"Look at that. Triple shield protection. Let's see how good that works against this." He pulled another gun from his left leg pocket and merged them together. Then he pushed something on the merging gun and pointed toward the triple balloons.

A brighter, thicker laser went toward the balloons and turned the exterior balloon red. Then the red exterior balloon separated from the other two and became smaller, like a fireball, about the size of a basketball. Mean Anzear took another shot and the red fire balloon went toward him very fast. That threw him onto the ground. At the same time, the fire in the forest disappeared. The other two balloons that covered Angika and Zeke were gone, too. Angika and Zeke hugged each other. They looked at good Anzear who was backing up slowly.

Anzear put his arms down. He walked toward mean Anzear who was lying on the ground. "Look at that monster. Am I that ugly, friends?" A screen popped up again in front of his chest and disappeared in a few seconds. He bent over and pulled a rhomb as big as the palm of his hand out of his chest. The rhomb looked like a crystal, but it wasn't shining. Then he held it with both hands close to the body lying on the ground. The crystal started to shine, but only in the direction of the body, creating a connection of light. All kinds of human, animal shapes and forms were changing and being sucked into the crystal rhomb. "He could be anything except a good human or earth creature. And he is not *I*, the real Anzear, either. Right, buddies?" Said Anzear.

"Then what is he? Who is he?" asked Angika, who was very confused.

"He looks like a shadow of a human now. Sometimes he changes to the shadow of a lizard. All this time, he was playing us," Zeke pointed out.

"I have a lot of explaining to do," said Anzear. "To you, to my Superiors, to Arl. But let's get him out of the water first before he turns into an amphibian."

Zeke couldn't take his eyes off Anzear, the imposter. "As far as his looks," continued Anzear pointing to the imposter, "I can't help you there. That is going to be a mystery for some time." The light connection between the rhomb and the fake Anzear stopped. A square box that looked like a crystal covered his whole body again. "Don' worry. He is fine. He is just inactive. In a short while, I will tell you who he is," said Anzear.

"I always hoped that Anzear we met didn't turn out to be a jerk. He had no reason to," said Angika. "You said let's go get Arl. I believe he's going to be okay. I can almost believe anything now," and she ran toward the lake. Zeke followed her and he started to take his shirt off and was ready to go into the lake when Anzear called him.

"Zeke, wait. He is going to be fine. I froze him. Actually, he did not literally freeze. It is like pausing a movie. He is not going to experience anything. He is just going to wake up," said Anzear as he was walking. He got close to the lake and didn't stop when he was inside the water.

"I knew it!" declared Zeke. "Anzear we knew wasn't afraid of the water. He even enjoyed it." Zeke and Angika followed with their eyes as Anzear disappeared into the lake. A couple of minutes went by.

"Come on. Come on," said Angika, pulling Zeke's arm.

"Something dark is coming out," said Zeke. "That's Arl's hair. That's Arl's head. Yeah!" He raised his right hand. He couldn't raise the left one. Angika was holding on to that one as tightly as though her hands were clamps. Like an antique statue, Arl was coming up on the surface. He wasn't moving. He stopped going up when his feet barely touched the surface of the water. Anzear couldn't be seen anywhere.

"Zeke, why isn't he moving?" asked Angika. "Anzear said he's going to be okay." Arl then started to move toward the shore, always barely touching the water's surface. He wasn't walking. He wasn't flying, either.

"He's moving like he is standing on an escalator," said Zeke. "He seems to still be frozen." Arl stopped moving right by the shore.

"What is up buddies?" asked a voice that came from behind the kids.

"Ah!" Angika turned her head. She released Zeke's arm, but grabbed him quickly by pulling him back. "Oh, Anzear, stop it!" said Angika after she released Zeke and both her shoulders went down.

"A joke. I am sorry I scared you," said Anzear. "Look behind you."

Zeke didn't have time to say anything. Angika turned her head again and there was Arl.

"You two look alright. You too Anzear. What happened to the other...? The last time I remember.... What happened to me?" asked Arl, trying to catch Angika who jumped up to give him a big hug.

"You're not even wet," said Angika. She let go of Arl. "Are you really Arl? What's the name of my cat?"

"Bora. Or snow-white. Hey, Zeke, buddy, don't ask me for your hairy dog. By the way, we have to find and save Pepe," said Arl, who gave Zeke a big hug, too.

"Yes, the creep that put Pepe and us in the balloons is now in a box: a crystal box. At least it looks like a crystal," said Zeke.

"Yes, Anzear took care of him. All this time, he used Anzear's identity to fool us," said Angika.

"Well, he almost did. It was almost impossible without the real Anzear," said Arl. "Thanks a lot, buddy. We owe you a big one."

"We are not done yet. Thank me later when we save Pepe and other Earth goodies," said Anzear.

"Are you feeling okay, Arl?" asked Angika.

"I feel great. Very light and fresh, and dry," said Arl, looking at his shirt.

"We're almost dry, too," said Zeke and he looked at Anzear. "Can we go to look for Pepe and the others now?"

"Yes, it's about time," said Angika. "Fortunately, I didn't bring my IPOD. It would have gotten all wet." She looked at Zeke and Arl. "Boys, do I look silly listening to the IPOD all the time?"

Arl and Zeke looked at each other. "A little," said Zeke.

"Really, Arl?" said Angika.

"I'm joking. I'll get one, too."

"And one for Pepe," said Arl. "I heard pets are happier and healthier if they listen to music."

"That is partially true," said Anzear. In theory for us, anyway," and he started to move toward the forest.

"In theory? Do you mean…?" Angika Started to ask.

"I will explain everything later," said Anzear.

There's a lot to be explained, thought Arl, following Zeke and Angika through the forest.

"Your forest is beautiful," said Anzear. "The whole Planet Earth needs a lot of work, though. Or maybe we are not used to it." Then he stopped in front of some thick bushes. He raised his left arm and the usual screen appeared in front of his chest. Arl was looking around, trying to make sense of all those lines and symbols that moved constantly. "Europe!" said Anzear, raising his right arm. The friends looked at each other. Anzear looked at them. Then he checked the screen again. "Eureka! I found it."

"Where? What?" asked Zeke, looking at the screen.

"Look! There," said Anzear. His left arm was pointing at some thick bushes. He pushed a couple of buttons on his left arm. Suddenly, from an almost fifty-foot wide area, all the bushes disappeared and a bare boulder showed up.

"How?" Zeke was looking around. "Where did they go?"

"It was just an illusion. A good one," said Anzear. "I noticed that on the screen that inside the boulder are a lot of habitants from your area. We need a plan for rescuing them, for placing them in their original homes. We will start with Pepe first."

"Good idea," said Angika.

"I will bring them to life. I will temporarily replace the balloons with cages. I don't understand why you created cages on Earth in the first place. Then you can come back with your Superiors to take care of the rest. I will go now and bring Pepe. Wait here, buddies.

You, too, Zeke," said Anzear when he saw Zeke following him.

Anzear walked toward the boulder. He didn't stop when he got closer to the stone edge. Instead, he turned into dust and disappeared.

"Another trick," said Angika. "The show never ends." A loud bark came from their left. Everybody knew that bark. It was Pepe running toward Zeke like a bullet.

"Oh, he's going to push me down, I know," said Zeke, as he squatted on his knees.

"Pepe, you look good. Wow!" Angika squatted on her knees, too.

"Finally," said Arl. "Now we are all together. Group hug?" Arl got down, too, and with their arms around each other, they created a human chain with Pepe in the middle.

"What are you doing? I do not know this move," said Anzear.

"It is a hug, group hug. A friendship hug," responded Arl, still smiling after seeing Pepe.

"It is not the handshake or the fists touching each other?" asked Anzear.

"Those too. I guess this is closer. Like when you have missed someone," explained Arl as he stood up.

"Interesting," said Anzear as he stretched his arms like he was grabbing somebody.

"Give me a hug," said Arl. "You are our friend, too."

"Yes, I am," said Anzear. Arl patted him on his shoulder and felt a metal sensation, then a leather one. Maybe a hairy one or a cloth sensation. Anzear wasn't moving. It was Arl's first close contact with Anzear. He never thought of what was under those unseen clothes. He wanted to ask him, but what to ask first? He had too many questions.

"Okay good friends. My mission is going to end pretty soon. I am not satisfied with our performance, but I am really satisfied with yours," said Anzear.

"Why? You helped us a lot," said Angika after she stood up.

"Let us walk and I will continue my explanation from where we left off. I do not think we are going to be interrupted again," said Anzear, and he started walking in the direction where the *trees with five leaves* were.

"Come on, friends," said Arl.

"Come on, Pepe," said Zeke. Pepe barked once like he approved.

"Let's see what happened with our trees," said Angika

"We did not come here to fight, to make a show of our power. We came here to explore," said Anzear as they were getting close to the trees.

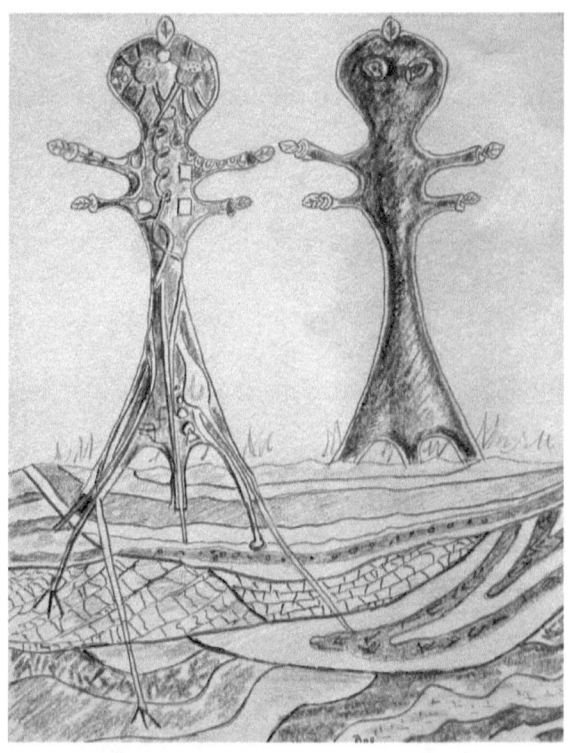

CHAPTER 16

"Still the same, not a leaf more, not a leaf less," said Angika. "They are never going to change," said Anzear. "And this is why." In a few seconds, a door opened from one of the trees, similar to a mummy's casket. The friends backed up one step, unable to believe their eyes. The tree had turned into a laboratory with items they had never seen before, either in school or anywhere else. "This is my tree laboratory," said Anzear. "Other trees are the same inside, but are controlled by two of my colleagues. You can see that they are not perfect trees. We didn't make more branches and a lot more leaves. This is our mistake. But it turned out that our mistake gave us a better answer for your planet."

Arl didn't know what to think about first. Everything was parading in his head, in an irregular order. Anzear looked weird, but some people look like that, which is why they got tricked.

"Relax, kids, I am your friend. We don't want to hurt anybody. We had a mission that our superiors gave us." Anzear paused briefly and then continued again. "Our people have four stages in their lives. We are in the first stage, just as you are. Your planet was getting hotter lately, and it caught the attention of our researchers. Anyway, they decided to first send a team with not much experience, like us, followed by experts. This was going to be like a science project for us. Our job was to get as much information as we could from your planet. Our first trip was to study the terrain. We chose your forest, a non-inhabited area. A few days earlier, we flew by the lake and the forest, and installed our trees that are equipped with everything to study and do tests. Instead of roots, there are tentacles that go deep into the ground to take samples and send them up for tests.

"Hey, Arl and Zeke, do you remember the news a few days ago that a fisherman saw a flying object?" said Angika.

"Yes," said Zeke, "I remember very well. We told Arl the story, too. Who would have thought that we were going to meet one of the crew members of that flying object?"

Anzear continued: "Each tree is being controlled by a crew member: two of my friends and me. We do that from a baby ship in the sky. We check the progress of each tree, save the test results, and send them to our mothership. We thought that our project was going to be jeopardized when we saw Arl paying a lot of attention to our tree-laboratories. One of my colleagues wanted to take action against Arl, but we didn't let him. We paralyzed him for a while. Our superiors are testing us for our patience, too. We decided to wait. Then Arl showed up again, this time with two more individuals: Zeke and Angika. We monitored everything you did, trying to figure out your intentions. Our friend messed up again. He created a poisonous fruit in the tree that he was monitoring, trying to poison Arl, but I had to intervene again. I created a vacuum that sucked you away from that tree. I did that in such a way that you wouldn't get hurt when you fell, Arl, and I gave you some energy just in case.

Arl remembered that he didn't feel anything after he woke up. Actually, he had felt really well, and energized. The big puzzle was being solved little by little. All the unanswered questions were being cleared up one by one.

"Now we know how the fruit disappeared," said Angika. "Wait a minute. All those eerie noises that I heard in my headphone over and over again, now we know the reason," said Angika, who put her right hand on her chest like she was trying to prevent her heart from falling to the ground.

"And those eerie noises that came from the ground. Actually they came from tree laboratories?" asked Zeke. "And what about the fence? Was that your team again?"

Even on Anzear's manikin-like face, some guilt was apparent. "Yes, it was the same hard-headed friend. If you can see, it is the same tree that produced the fruit.

I, and one of my friends, were sure that your intentions were good. You wanted those trees to grow like the others. Our other friend was hard to convince. That's why he acted up again, and broke the fence. Then we decided to meet with you, risking the success of our mission. We did that to prevent those kinds of people from hurting your planet. Because it was my idea to meet you, they wanted me to have the biggest risk. But I had confidence in you three. The problem was how was I going to appear to you? I had to find a way. So I decided to create a collage of your appearances."

The kids were observing each other like it was the first time they had ever seen each other. Then they started to figure out the collage. Arl looked simultaneously at Anzear, Angika and Zeke. He started thinking, obviously, Anzear (or Sirus) got the braid from

Angika's looks, and a little bit of her eyelids. But he put the braid in front of his head, and Arl remembered that he had flipped it back when he met them the first time. Looking at Anzear's (or Sirus's) hair, he could see that it was straight and dark, which he might have gotten from him (Arl). Then Arl thought, "Anzear's hair also becomes reddish and curly. His eyes are very light blue, which reminds me of Zeke. So I got an idea of the Sirus look, but his clothes seemed like they were made by a crazy designer. Obviously, he didn't have much information about that. His voice had the same tonality. Overall, he could blend into some urban neighborhoods, where groups of youngsters change their appearance, using any color of the rainbow, and an alien can find his home there, just by being different."

"You don't feel hot with that long-sleeved jacket, and long pants?" asked Angika and her eyes widened a little. "Are you wearing a mask to look like us?"

"No, no mask," replied Anzear.

"Then, what is that, magic?" Angika asked again.

"I don't know the meaning of your magic process yet, and I cannot explain the process of visual transformation. I am sorry, but I am not authorized. As far as long sleeves and long pants, they are a good cover-up. My temperature is normal. Normal for me," said Anzear.

"How did you come up with the name Anzear?" asked Zeke.

Anzear paused again. "Let's make that a solving riddle. I am sure you are going to solve it."

"Can we still call you Anzear then?" Zeke asked again.

"Yes, no problem, but still concentrate on solving the name riddle," continued Anzear.

"Can you give us a hint about the name?" asked Angika.

"A hint? Let me find out the meaning of the word *hint*." Anzear paused again for a few seconds, and then continued. "Yes, it is similar to my appearance. That is good enough."

The kids took a deep breath. That was one thing they surely didn't need, thought Arl – another stressful thing for their brain. *Let's forget that for a while,* thought Arl, *and concentrate on the main things.*

"Are there other ships in the sky that spy for your planet? Like the jerk that tried to destroy us?" asked Arl.

"I am not informed about that. There might be more. I know that they go everywhere they can in the galaxy to collect information. I know that they have only scientific purposes, to prevent any cosmic disaster, to know our galaxy neighbors, etc. As far as the jerk, I feel really embarrassed. That's my hard-headed friend. He went too far the last time.

Anzear paused longer than before, made a 360-degree turn with his head, and continued.

"I think our work for your planet is done for now. We know that your climate is changing, but we saw the concern of the people that live here. That gives us hope that you are going to act quickly, carefully and responsibly. You are great human kids." Then, Anzear pushed something on his arm, which appeared to be a button, waited a little while, and continued again. "I have confirmation to take you kids for a quick trip in our ship, and then for a ride. What do you think?"

Arl looked at Zeke, then Angika. This was a dream come true for him! Was this really happening? They were talking to an alien or an extraterrestrial being, and he was even their friend. Now, he was asking them to visit their ship, even to take a ride. This was a dream for every human, especially for a kid, but at the same time, it could be very dangerous. It could be a lot of fun, but this could be the last time they were going to see their sun, their lake, their forest, their town and their families. But the power of curiosity, the power of the unknown was very strong. Arl's naivety, his willingness to trust the others, his innocence and his pure soul, freed him from the fear.

"What do you think Zeke?" asked Arl. Zeke couldn't speak a word. "Hey, Angika, one for all, and all for one?"

"Three G's," said Angika.

"Three G's," said Zeke.

"You can bring the dog, too," said Anzear.

"Three G's and a half," said Zeke, including Pepe. The three friends made a vow, like always, with their palms down. Anzear approached, looking amazed.

"What is that," he asked.

"This is a sign of close friendship and commitment," said Arl.

"Can I put my hand on yours, too?" asked Anzear. "You are my friends. Good friends."

The kids looked at each other, and all at the same time said, "Yes, you can." Anzear stretched his hand out, looking very excited.

"We have to make a circle five feet in diameter," said Anzear. "Are you ready?"

"Yes," responded the kids again at the same time. Their hearts started to beat faster and faster. Arl felt like his was almost going to pop out of his little chest.

"Be calm, relax; it will not take long," said Anzear. He made the rhomb sign again, looking up in the sky. In a few seconds, an object that looked like a cone was standing still, a few feet above their head. The object was really shiny, and it was a mixture of colors, dominated by a warm gray. The kids held hands, really tight. Zeke held Angika's hand with one of his hands, the other hand was holding Pepe close to his chest. They didn't hear any noise at all. "This is our baby ship," said Anzear. He clicked something again on his arm vest, and in a few seconds, a vacuum was created. The kids noticed that they were a few inches above the ground.

"Are we flying?" asked Angika and her braids went up like an antenna. Yes, we are," she answered herself. Unconsciously, they closed their eyes, and when they opened them, they found themselves surrounded by strange apparatuses.

"Welcome to my ship, my friends. Take a seat, relax. Anzear sat down first. When he said to take a seat, he meant sitting in the air, not on a chair. The kids were skeptical at first, but when they saw Anzear sitting calmly, they also attempted to sit slowly, feeling like they were going to fall down. But they didn't. In front of them appeared a forest in a satellite view and then in a bird's view, and finally, an up-close view. What they saw first were the famous *five leaves trees*. They saw different views of the same tree. First a natural view, which could be seen by a regular eye. The other view was the transparent one, making it possible to see both the outside and the inside parts of the tree. After that we looked at different views that showed tentacles inside the ground, coming from the trunk of all three trees.

"They're supposed to be roots, but obviously, their purpose is different," said Angika. "Look at those scriptures in the different apparatuses that we don't understand." Her eyes were bigger than usual. The views weren't on any screen. They just appeared in front of them.

"The whole lake can't water those trees," continued Arl. "And certainly we couldn't with our simple buckets." Then from the trees came another view. In front of Arl appeared his house. Then he saw Grandpa Toke. He was working in the garden. He seemed close enough to talk to. Then another view showed Angika's house, which was known for the many different kinds of flowers they had. And last, but not least, Zeke's house, which was built all in stones gathered from a mountain not far away from their town. They could even see Pepe's miniature house, too. Pepe, scared, looked more like a toy dog than a real one. He barked with excitement when he saw a familiar view. The kids were really excited to see their houses too, in a pilot or satellite view. Their town looked especially beautiful from up there. All this time, Anzear was playing with his apparatuses. Then in a second, their town became a dot. After a few seconds, they could see a ball. That was the Earth. It reminded them of the pictures of Earth they had seen in some science books. You couldn't measure the joy in their faces. To everybody's amazement, Pepe was as calm as he could be. He didn't make a sound. Maybe Anzear had something to do with that.

Then a message appeared in front of them. They could read it. It said, "I am sorry for trying to sabotage your work. Gaus orb Arl, Gaus orb all."

"Gaus orb, Arl? What does '*orb Arl*' mean?" asked Angika.

"That is for you three from my hard-headed friend, especially for Arl," explained Anzear. "Orb means that you and him are in the same circle in your language, *friends*."

"I thought he was shut down," said Angika. "You're going to let him get away with all that happened?"

"Seeing that one of us had bad intentions, made the Superiors realize that we have work to do in our civilization, that we are not perfect. We still have some weak spots. I have to add, though, that none of our weapons cause permanent damages. Neither can they hurt or kill somebody," said Anzear.

As far as the Earth, the Superiors left a message for you." The kids were expecting to see the message, but instead, they heard a deep voice.

"Greetings, young Earthlings! We apologize for our young one, for his dangerous behavior. We thought we got rid of 'the jealousy' feeling in our society, but the miracles of your planet confused our young one. He made the case that "humans don't appreciate what they have. They do not deserve it. Humans are polluting the water. We have to use artificial water on our planet." Then he continued, "Humans abuse animals, forests, each other, etc. He thought that you were some of those abusive Earth creatures. We know that on Earth there are too many negative creatures, but when we see young kids like you, we have hope. We know now that you are going in the right direction. We always are going to keep a close look at Earth, because our planet depends on you astronomically. But we are not going to intervene. We are going to leave it up to you. We are going to be your last hope. Good luck, our friends!" The kids raised their hands like they were waving to somebody.

Then, another message appeared: "Greetings from Krilon. Krilon orb all of you."

"That is my other friend, and I apologize for all of us, for not revealing ourselves. I am sure we are going to meet again in the future, under different circumstances. My time is up. We have to go down. Don't forget the name riddle."

The ship went down with a speed that made the earth get bigger, like a balloon being filled with air. Arl didn't want it to end.

"I am sorry, buddies. I wish I could stay with you longer, but I already surpassed my orders. Forgive my friends and me again for not revealing our identity. We are not authorized to do it, but I promise that I am going to ask the superiors for you kids to come and visit us on our home planet. So, we are going to see each other pretty soon and maybe on a superior level."

CHAPTER 17

Arl didn't feel that they arrived back in the forest. It got black for a second, but when he opened his eyes, they were standing on the ground, and the baby ship was gone. It had all happened so fast. Arl was thinking *did it really happen*? When Arl saw Anzear with a weird look, but almost like them, for a moment, everything seemed fake, but what they saw earlier was real. The trees were not real. The ship was real. *Can they handle the truth? Yes, they can. Yes, they will.*

"Did you three forget to solve something?" asked Anzear.

"Your look is our collage. Regarding your hint, the name should be our collage, too," said Arl. "Your name has six letters. We are three people. We divide three out of six, and we have two letters for each of our names. *AR* L, *AN* GIKA, *ZE* KE."

"Aranze, Arzean, Anzear. We got you," said Angika happily. The conversation helped them forget for a short time where they had been a few minutes earlier.

"One thing is bothering me," said Anzear.

"What is that?" asked Arl, anxious and still shocked.

"If Pepe gets, hot do you eat him in any way? I know you eat hot dogs, but I don't know how and which kind of dogs. I feel really bad knowing Pepe, who is such a precious creature," said Anzear. The kids started laughing loudly. That helped them release the extra pressure that had built up in their heads.

"Let's make that a solving riddle for you," said Arl. "We assure you, we don't eat dogs. That includes Pepe. We call them family pets. They live with us, usually until they leave this world, if you know what I mean," finished Arl.

"My mistake, but I made you laugh. I am glad I got a chance to know you kids. But now, it is time to go." Anzear extended his right arm. Arl did likewise, and Angika did the same thing. Zeke grabbed Pepe, stretched his paw out, then his arm, and all promised to be friends forever. "See you soon. *Live for leaves*. Orb." Anzear walked a few steps, made the rhomb sign again, and then just disappeared into thin air. The kids were getting used to that now. They looked up in the sky, trying to catch sight of Anzear and the flying object, but nothing moved in the sky. The sky looked quiet like nothing had happened there, but our friends knew otherwise. Then suddenly, a moving cloud appeared. It was moving, making circles and lines.

"What might that be?" asked Zeke. Pepe barked once, looking up in the sky. And, all of a sudden, the kids could read something in the sky. In gigantic letters it said, *LIVE FOR LEAVES, 3G'S + 1G.*

"That's Anzear!" they all exclaimed in a chorus. Then another figure was being created.

"That looks like a banana," said Angika.

"No, more like a squash," said Zeke. Pepe barked twice. "He has his own opinion," joked Zeke looking at Pepe.

"It looks like he solved the riddle," said Arl. "The figure is a hot dog. Anzear even created the steam."

"He really is a good alien. Now he's gone," said Angika.

"Yes, he is," agreed both Arl and Zeke. Pepe barked once, meaning that he agreed, too. The letters stayed in the sky for a minute or two, and then they started to dissipate until they disappeared. The sky got clear, but our friends were still looking up in the sky, like they were expecting more messages. Pepe barked again. Pepe's bark reminded them of the ground they were standing on. In other words, it brought them *down to earth*. They were looking around bewildered. Something was missing. While looking up in the sky, the kids didn't notice that the trees with five leaves had disappeared. They all ran to see what was left. They saw nothing, only regular dirt, the fence, and their tools, as though nothing had happened there. If that was the first thing that Arl saw that day, he was going to be very surprised, but he had seen a lot of unseen things. So, that just added another surprise in a day full of surprises.

"That means that their mission is done, like Anzear, or Sirus, confirmed," said Arl. "We really need a good break, pals. Don't you think?"

"We sure do!" agreed Angika.

"I guess we have a lot of explaining to do tomorrow," said Zeke. Pepe agreed again, barking, and wagging his tail. He became himself again.

"Our mission here is done, too," said Arl. "We have to continue our mission somewhere else where we will all be needed. Like, Real "*3 G's*." Arl felt that he was talking like a grownup. That had been happening a lot lately, and it felt good. They were feeling more important, more valuable.

"LIVE FOR LEAVES," said both Angika and Zeke. Then, the kids grabbed their things that they had left by the *trees with five leaves*, and walked slowly, but very happily toward the lake. There, they got the rest of their things and fastened them to their bikes. Zeke put Pepe into his cargo rack this time. The kids looked at the lake for a moment, as though saying goodbye, hopped on their bikes, and started to ride. They didn't say a word all the way home. Time after time, they looked up in the sky, as if they expected to see something. They were each deep in their own thoughts. Even Pepe didn't bark like he usually did. So much had happened that day. They couldn't put it into words, until tomorrow. They hugged each other tightly before they went to their own houses.

"Thank you pals," said Arl, "for sticking with me the whole time. Sorry for all the trouble. I should apologize to your families, too, when they find out what happened today."

"No, thank you for making us a part of this," said Zeke. "Even Pepe, t*he hot dog*, is thankful. From now on, he's going to be a *hot dog*, not just a *dog*." They were all giggling, thinking again of Anzear's question.

"I guess our families are going to be proud of us," and you are going to be their favorite," Angika said to Arl. "So let's get some sleep. We're going to have a big day tomorrow."

The kids left for their houses one by one. The town still looked the same, unaware of the very special events that had taken place that day. The city wanted some sleep, just like the kids, so it threw on its dark blanket, and lights started to appear one by one around the city like stars. Arl saw his mom in the kitchen, and ran to her and gave her a big, long hug. Then, another big, long hug for Grandpa Toke, and he went to his room.

"Wow, what was that all about? He missed us so much after being gone for only part of the day?"Briza said to Grandpa Toke.

"I don't know, Briza, he looked different," said GT. "We will ask him tomorrow."

EPILOGUE

The next day, Arl woke up as usual. He dragged himself to the bathroom, and then he took his time eating breakfast. He wasn't in a hurry. He wasn't going anywhere for a while.

"Finally, you got tired of going to the forest?" asked his mom.

"No, we're not going today," said Arl.

GT was reading the morning newspaper. "Look at that!" he said, pointing to an article in the paper. "Another sighting. A flying object has been seen again, but this time it wrote something in the sky. It drew something too. Something like a banana or cucumber. They can't figure it out. They're going to send the photos to a laboratory for a clearer view."

"Really? What did they write?" asked Briza. "Let's check the TV." She turned on the TV morning news.

"They wrote '*Live for leaves*" and drew that banana-looking figure," said GT.

Then the news reporter's voice filled the room. "Breaking news. Another sighting. This time it was very strange because they wrote something in our language, followed by a drawing. It could be a prank, but the experts say that the speed of the flying object exceeded by far the speed of any of our flying machines. And it was seen in the same area again, flying over the forest, by the lake, in Krasta town." Both GT and Briza looked at Arl. He wasn't surprised. He had a guilty look in his face. He was going to tell his family about his adventure anyway, but somehow the news made it easy for him. If there hadn't been a sighting, nobody would have believed him or his friends. Maybe nobody was going to believe that they had seen and spoken to one of the crewmember who was in that ship, or who hung out with them for that matter. But, they had proof. They were the only ones that knew the story of the drawing. Only they knew the slogan *LIVE FOR LEAVES*. He has the photos of the strange trees. Actually, Anzear did the kids a big favor by promoting their idea. Every big TV channel was going to talk about this story. Later, they were going to interview the three kids about it. What better advertisement could they ask for? Everybody was going to be involved. The media getting involved made Arl very happy. He couldn't wait to talk with Angika and Zeke about it. All they would have to do was answer questions and talk about their ideas in front of the camera. Arl already was envisioning thousands and thousands of kids and adults spreading around the word to achieve the *GET GREENER GOAL*. Arl smiled.

"What's so funny?" asked Briza. "You know something about this? And that's funny?"

"Yes, Mom. It's a long story. That day when I went to the lake with Grandpa, I noticed some strange looking trees. And ..." Arl continued the story, and was amused by his mother's changing expressions. Her eyebrows were going up and down. Sometimes, there was a smile in her face, but most of the time, she just looked astonished. GT seemed more relaxed.

"That's my boy," said GT. Mom gave Arl another hug, pulling him tight, like she was afraid she was going to lose him.

"We are raising good kids, aren't we, Briza?" said GT.

"Yes, we are GT," said Briza, smiling. "Dad is going to be very proud of you, Arl. You deserve the volcanic stones."

Arl felt very complimented. He was wondering how Angika and Zeke's mornings were going. He bet they were having a full morning, too. A lot of new experiences were waiting ahead. One of them was that they would be planting three trees in the same spots where the *trees with five leaves* were. "It's going to be a busy summer", Arl was thinking. "It's going to be a green one. It's going to be beautiful."

THE END

Arian Zene

Artist, writer, dad, earth lover...

Arian lives with his family in Michigan, USA. He used pens and brushes since he was a kid, back in Albania, Europe. This time he combined these two together to create this science fiction story, painting with words the vitality of the new generation...

www.ingramcontent.com/pod-product-compliance
Lightning Source LLC
Chambersburg PA
CBHW022246290526
45785CB00015B/305